Christians Incompatible with Christ

How Do Christians Approach
the Issue of Homosexuality?

By Rev. Gary L. Hakes

Contact the author at IncompatibleChristians@gmail.com.

ISBN-13: 978-1519512581

ISBN-10: 1519512589

Dedication

This book is dedicated to all those sexually diverse persons, including gay, lesbian, and transgendered, who have suffered prejudice, rejection, or any condemnation by those who call themselves "Christian." People who say and do such things prove by their behavior that they are not Christian. Jesus taught again and again that he did not come to condemn. Furthermore, he never had any kind of a teaching against such persons.

I, as one who claims to be Christian, apologize to one and all of you.

— Gary

About the Author

The Reverend Gary L. Hakes studied at Ohio Wesleyan University, National College for Christian Workers, Alfred School of Theology, Wesley School of Theology, and Syracuse University, earning a Bachelor's degree, a Masters Degree in Theology, and doing doctoral work on Religion and Mass Society.

Reverend Hakes served as a pastor in churches in Missouri, Pennsylvania, and New York State from 1951 to 2002. He began his research into sexuality in 1957 in response to questions from youth group members and developed a sexuality course for youth and parents in partnership with Planned Parenthood. As a result, Reverend Hakes became a part of the education section for Planned Parenthood. His studies included seminars from Masters and Johnson and Drs. Noam and Beryl Chernick of Canada. In 1972, the United Methodist Church developed a curriculum for teaching human sexuality and Reverend Hakes was trained by Dr. Cortoy and commissioned by his Annual Conference to be a sex educator for the Conference churches. He became chair of the Conference committee and was part of the first group to be educated about HIV/Aids by a group of experts in California.

When appointed to the Seneca Falls, NY, church, Reverend Hakes became a member of the Board of Directors of the Geneva, NY, Planned Parenthood and later served as its president. He continued his education concerning sexuality issues with and programs presented by the University of Massachusetts, Syracuse University, the University of Pennsylvania, and the University of Virginia.

When a violent incident in his church made him aware of issues related to homosexuality, Reverend Hakes began a study of some 100 authors on all sides of the issue. To organize his thoughts, he wrote a lengthy paper in which he concluded that homosexuals were as normal and moral as heterosexuals. In response to the paper, the bishop appointed Reverend Hakes to lead seminars for the clergy of the area, and the paper was used in college classes across the U.S. From that time on, much of his ministry involved counseling with gay men and women who sought him out.

This book is a result of Reverend Hakes' frustration with his church that declares, "homosexuality is incompatible with Christian teaching," while Jesus never taught any such thing. The church betrays Christ with this teaching. Such "Christians" are incompatible with Christ.

Acknowledgements

This book would not have been possible without the support of two people in particular.

My sincere thanks to my editor, Katy O'Grady of D & O Creative Group, for her patience and organizational skills. Her work helped me to bring this book to publication, which has been a goal of mine for quite some time.

And my profound thanks to my daughter Heather, whose belief in this project, persistence, and dedication helped make the finished product a reality.

Table of Contents

Introduction 1

Chapter 1: Experience 5

Chapter 2: Experience Goes to Work 29

Chapter 3: "The Word of God" 37

Chapter 4: Biblical Background 51

Chapter 5: Misusing Scriptural Texts 79

Chapter 6: Tradition 108

Chapter 7: Reason 134

Bibliography 163

Notes 166

Introduction

How do Christians approach the issue of homosexuality?

To begin to answer that question, one must define what one means by "Christian." Although all Christians may claim to follow the way of Jesus, the paths they choose to follow can be very different. There are those who center on personal salvation while others strive for the salvation of all. The huge problem here is that none of us is in charge of salvation. That is God's work. And, of course, there are varieties in between those approaches.

There are those who consider all Scripture equal and directly from the mouth of God. There are also those who understand the Old Covenant texts as a developmental theology that gradually prepared the people for the culmination of the coming of Christ. These Christians see the New Covenant as superseding the Old. There are Christians who have a need to force others to believe as they do and Christians who accept people as they are and love them and care for them and allow

God to work in their lives. There are Christians who tell other Christians that they are "going to Hell!" Many types of people call themselves Christians. This writer simply refers to Christians as those who follow the teachings and way of Jesus, the Christ.

To approach the issue of homosexuality, I use John Wesley's Quadrilateral. I chose Wesley's Quadrilateral because of what Wesley accomplished in dealing with tough issues during the 1700s: the condition of the miners, the widows and orphanages, alcohol issues, child labor laws, children working as chimney sweeps, slavery, medical concerns, and more. His approach to handling these issues is said to have kept England from experiencing the kind of revolution that occurred in France.

This approach is called a quadrilateral because Wesley used four categories—Scripture, tradition, experience, and reason—in making a decision concerning an issue. Because I am thoroughly convinced that our experience is so powerful that it colors everything we think, do, and read, I start with experience first. Chapter 1 shares my own experience and how it has affected my life and decision making; my approach to Scripture, tradition, and reasoning; and my belief system.

Chapter 2 explores my work with the church and my introduction to sex education. Dealing with these various concerns led into discussions about homosexuality. In chapter 3, I explore what is meant by "the Word of God." Here we see why Jesus told us not to get into issues of doctrine. As a result of neglecting his teaching, we developed doctrines defining "The Word of God," "The Nature of God," "Original Sin,"

"Inspiration," "Inerrancy," and many more, which resulted in heresies and terrible judgments and punishments.

Chapter 4 provides Biblical background that challenges our assumptions about the Bible. Rather than following the teachings of Jesus, too many have followed the way of the Pharisees and turned Christianity into another form of legalism, as opposed to being guided by grace. The Bible's very first story (after the creation stories) warns us to stay away from the fruit of the judgment tree. Let us approach the Bible with facts rather than assumptions, and with new eyes. Let us come to the Scripture without looking for authority to support our biases, but rather to see it as it is and for what it has to reveal.

Chapter 5 examines texts in both the New and Old Testaments that have been used against gay people. In point of fact, the word "homosexual" was not formulated until 1869 and was not in any Bible until 1952, in the RSV of all places! Since 1989, that translation has gone back to the correct translation of Scripture. Furthermore, the definition of homosexuality has changed several times since it originated in 1869. It has gone all the way from a "sick practice," to a "preference" for the same sex, to a natural "emotional and physical" need for the same sex. I address issues stemming from translation and cultural bias and the problem that some use Scripture as a yardstick to measure by while others regard Scripture as an inner principle that informs, grows, and matures amid changes and challenges.

Chapter 6 addresses tradition, the third part of Wesley's Quadrilateral, and considers our Christology and the tradition of the

Church concerning sexuality. This information will come as a surprise to many readers.

Reason is Wesley's fourth standard. Having explored the standards of Scripture, tradition, and experience, we now consider reason in making a decision about the issue of homosexuality. Chapter 7 incorporates current research in psychoneuroendocrinology and biology regarding the origin of sexual orientation in human beings, proving that homosexuality is biological, natural, not a preference, not a choice.

Have you analyzed your theology, your Christology? Do you understand why you have your kind of "Christianity?" Does it really follow the teachings of Jesus?

Chapter 1

Experience

Our experience powerfully affects everything we think, do, and read. I share my own experience to illustrate its impact on my life, my decisions, and my belief system.

I was born in a different era. My family lived in a very narrow, winding valley squeezed between two very steep, high, forested hills in upstate New York. We used horses for farm work and hauling our milk to the local dairy. We had neither electricity nor plumbing in the early years. As a result, of course, we had to carry our water from a spring a few hundred yards away and we had a fancy three-seater outhouse. We did have a kitchen sink that drained into a bucket.

The man who married and impregnated my mother was never a father to me, nor to any of his nine offspring. He was a drunken, brawling womanizer who was seldom home. When he was at home, life was nothing but pure terror. Until I was about eight years old, I spent many nights curled up in the cupboard under the kitchen sink, praying that he would not find me when and if he came home sometime during the night. He tried to kill me three times that I can recall. I will not use his name, but will refer to him as the sadist.

In his first attempt, the sadist tried to run over my mother and me with his car when I was very young. The second time, I was about four years old and did not get my snowsuit off fast enough to satisfy him. As a result, he lifted me face up in the air and was going to break my back over the back of a chair. My mother rushed over and pushed him off balance so that he had to drop me to try to save himself from a bad fall. She ended up a bloody mess on the floor in the corner of the next room. The third time he tried to kill me, I was about 10 years old. I was in the outhouse when he came home drunk. He asked where I was and when told, he got out his Marlin rifle and started shooting at the outhouse. Obviously, the first shot missed me and I immediately hit the floor and rolled out the door. The other two bullets went through right where I had been.

As a result of everyone knowing who and what my "father" was, as well as my being referred to as a "hick" from out in the hills, I was teased at school for a while. I soon learned that I had no one on whom I could depend for help, so I learned to fight. Not long after that, no bullies would bother anyone in my school. But it wasn't just the bullies in school who were offensive. The good Christian parents of some of my friends did not want their children playing with "those Hakes boys." As a result of those kinds of experiences, I decided in first grade that I was going to be just the opposite of the beast who married my mother. Furthermore, because I experienced what it was like to be mistreated, ostracized, and bullied, I came to empathize deeply for and with anyone who is treated unfairly. It was imprinted into my very being to fight such cruel behavior for the rest of my life.

The sadist was an ironworker, a welder who could weld metals that most other welders would not even attempt. Some of his projects included working on skyscrapers in New York City, putting cells in prisons, and being in charge of the ironwork for the support of the concrete in the Mt. Morris Dam and the iron framework in the construction of a huge A&P warehouse facility. This is another way of saying that he earned very good money for that era; however, he spent his paycheck buying drinks for his buddies on Friday nights. Often, not enough money was left for fuel for heat or enough food to eat, let alone the mortgage payment. Fortunately, my mother knew how to fry burdock greens, cook milkweed, use the roots of Queen Ann's Lace, cook dandelion greens, collect berries and nuts, and more. But winters were more than difficult. In the cold weather, my mother, brother, and I would huddle together in a big chair with a blanket around us, trying to keep in the body heat to prevent ourselves from freezing. This was upstate New York, not Florida! We often ate oatmeal three times a day, without milk or sugar. We sold milk and butter to the neighbors for a little money for essentials.

When I was eight, my mother was taken to a sanitarium more than 100 miles away to try to recuperate from tuberculosis. While she was there, my brother, sister, and I were transferred from one family to another. I had problems concentrating at school because I would often find myself thinking about my mother so far away and praying that God would heal her. A lot of good my praying did. When I was 11, after three years away, she died. A very religious uncle came to see us before going to the funeral. He put his hand on my shoulder and said "This is all God's will, and you are the man of the family now."

I thought to myself, "If this is God's will, I hate God. Furthermore, you've got to be one of the stupidest men alive." No 11-year-old is ready to be the man of the family.

After my mother died, the sadist went off to Montana to play cowboy. My brother, sister, and I were switched from relative to relative for the next three years. I do not know just how long the sadist was in Montana, but when I was 12, my brother and I were invited to spend July with him and his new partner, Lois. They had had a baby girl in May, named Lillian. One afternoon, while he was at work on the Mt. Morris Dam, I was sitting with Lois in the living room, talking. It was a hot, humid, still day and the front door was open so more air could come through the screen door. Lillian was lying in her bassinet nearby. All of a sudden, a man and woman rushed in the front door. The man rushed right past me and tossed a pile of money on the dining room table while the woman grabbed Lillian, and they were gone.

Lois started screaming and didn't stop for days. I spent the next 42 years looking for Lillian. In 1989, one of my sisters received a call at work from someone who said she was doing research on the Hakes family. She wanted permission to call my sister Robin at home to talk more in detail about the family. Robin agreed and gave her the unlisted number. The woman turned out to be Lillian, now known as Sandi. For most of those 42 years, except for Lois and her husband, only my brother and I had known of Lillian's existence. When Lois was dying of cancer, my sister Robin helped take care of her. Just before she died, Lois told Robin about Lillian. Had she not done so, Robin would not have been able to give Lillian the information she needed when she called. Robin immediately called another sister, who then contacted me. Since I knew the story, I called Lillian and related just what had happened so many years ago. Within two weeks, we had the first and only family reunion so that "Sandi" could meet her biological family. This experience of Lillian being stolen taught me that one cannot take anything for granted. There are all kinds of dynamics that can take place and change everything.

The sadist would never allow us to go to church because he said it was "filled with hypocrites." He knew because he claimed to have met them all in the bars Friday and Saturday nights. A couple of years after my mother died, I was living with relatives when, after chorus rehearsal in school one day, my music teacher asked me if I would come and sing in the choir at the Methodist Church where he was choir director. I told him I did not believe in God and that, if there was a God, I hated him.

"Well, you have a right to your beliefs, but I really wish you could come and help me out," he said.

In hopes of escaping this uncomfortable situation, I replied, "If I do come and sing, what do I do before and after we sing? Can I bring my comic books to have something to read?"

"You can if you are discreet," he answered. "Don't let anyone know what you are doing."

I agreed to try it. This meant that I had to walk some three miles each way to choir rehearsal on Wednesday evenings and again on Sunday morning.

I do not recall how long the comic book reading went on, but I had overheard conversations at church about the pastor's education. I had heard someone say that the preacher not only went to college, he even went several more years to seminary. One thing that I did appreciate was education and I believed my teachers had given me something to live for as I studied various subjects in school. Maybe I should listen to this guy, I thought. My ears would perk up when I heard him talk about Jesus and his teachings. The teachings of Jesus gave me a whole different perspective on the world. Jesus' message that he did not come to condemn and that his followers were not to condemn was a whole new concept. Forgiving and reconciling went even further.

"This is the way things ought to be," I thought to myself. "If people lived like this, what a different world it would be!" I was baptized and joined the church.

I started reading the Bible from the beginning to the end. A member at church had told me, "God wrote the Bible and every word in it is true, unchanging, and God never makes any mistakes."

When I got to Exodus, Leviticus, and Numbers, it was like trudging through wet cement. I thought, "If this is what God is like, I do not want any part of Him or this religion." However, I was never one to quit before I accomplish what I set out to do. I struggled through to the New Testament and the whole atmosphere seemed to change. I later discovered that I was not alone in this feeling. In the midst of all this, my pastor asked me to teach the second-graders in church school, when I was only 13! I couldn't believe it when I heard myself say, "Yes!" And that is when I really started to learn.

When I was 15, the sadist had married Lois and moved to a village some 20 miles away. I thought we should try to be a family again, so I rode my bicycle over the hills and found where they were living. I persuaded Lois that we should all be living together as a family and she agreed to talk to her husband about the prospect. Lois sent word by another aunt that it was agreed that we might try living together. This aunt came and picked up my brother and me to go and live with them.

The place where we lived was a group of six round tourist cabins that had been rented out in the past to travelers passing through, with a small office building out front. Lois and her husband lived in the small office building near the highway and my brother and I lived in one of the unheated cabins that sat in a semi-circle behind the office. The location was just south of town, opposite a huge auction building.

Not too long after moving to this community, I went to the Methodist church in town. I no sooner entered the nave of the church when I noticed that all of the men were in suits and many of the women had furs wrapped around their shoulders. I was wearing my plaid shirt and overalls. Fortunately, this church had an aisle along the back with a seating area in an alcove behind that aisle. I chose a seat back there, right near the door so I could escape as soon as the service was over. I was feeling very much out of my element. Unfortunately, the head usher was at the exit before I could get there. As I tried my best to get out the door, he stopped me with a hand on my shoulder.

"In this church, we honor God by wearing our best clothes to church," he said.

"I don't know why you go to church, but I go to worship God," I replied, "and I am wearing my best clothing." I left, humiliated and angry.

One day at school that week, I was called into the principal's office. On the way there, I kept asking myself, "What on earth did I do now?"

"Don't worry, you are not in trouble," the principal said as I entered the office. "Someone came into my office with two brand-new suits that he thought might fit you if you would accept them. He wants to remain anonymous. Are you willing to try them on and accept them if they fit?"

"I have been wearing hand-me-downs all my life," I responded. "Something new would be a change." I tried the suits on and they did fit.

That experience taught me to be very careful about quick judgments. Time and time again throughout life, people with whom I have had confrontations or disagreements have become some of my best, most loyal friends. I learned to let time, thinking, and kindness work its way. Don't let disagreements get in the way of wonderful possibilities.

Soon after joining that church, I started going to a Sunday morning class for youth. One morning, the teacher handed out a questionnaire that had been given to her by the pastor. I filled it out and forgot about it. During the next week, the pastor's son, who was in my class, came up to me in school and told me that his father wanted to see me in his office after school.

After school, I went to his office and upon being offered a chair to be seated, he said, "I read the questionnaire that you filled out in class

Sunday morning and it looks like to me that God is calling you to be a pastor."

I started laughing. "How could God want me?"

"Just look at how you have answered these questions," he said. "You are exactly who God needs for these times. You had better go home and pray about this."

That was the start of a long afternoon and night. I went home and began praying. I make an effort here to describe what happened; however, any words I use here cannot really convey the experience. A presence filled the room. I talked with God and gave all the reasons why I was not qualified to be a pastor. Not only that, I did not want to be a pastor. I liked to be liked and I knew that I would have to take stands on issues that would not be popular and would cause people to be upset with me. That was the last thing I wanted. I had had enough of people not liking me. But responses to my arguments kept coming back at me in very strong impressions. They were so real that they were like vocalized words, although they were not. There was no audible voice, and yet I felt very understandable perceptions. This went on all night long, almost until sunup. I developed a very clear understanding that I was to be a pastor, like it or not. Every time I think of Jacob anxiously waiting all night for his wronged brother, Esau, at the Jabbock River, I am reminded of this "call."

The next day, I went to talk to the pastor about this experience and my decision. My huge concern was money. College and seminary would cost a lot of money and I did not have two pennies to rub together nor any place to get any financial help. I told him of my concern.

"Oh, are you telling me that you don't have the faith that God will help you to accomplish this?" he said.

My first feeling was to be offended, but after thinking about what he said, I felt he had a point. My next feeling was that I needed to accept that this was going to happen and that I had to get busy to do my best to be part of its happening. I needed to find a job and I needed to start preparing myself.

I studied for my license to preach through Emory University and received my license in 1951. My pastor had a cooperative parish of seven churches. He put me to work sharing in the preaching and in working with youth groups in the churches. With this work, I had two years of hands-on ministry before going to college.

Because college would require so much money, I started looking for somewhere to work. I went to every single place of business in and around the village looking for work, but I could find no job of any kind. That is, I went to every single place but one. There was a very small grocery store known as a "Red and White" that I passed on my walk to school and I knew it was just too small to be hiring anyone. But one afternoon, while walking home, with my arms loaded with books, I heard someone yell, "Hey! You!" I could see no one around except a man standing on the steps of this little store across the street. He was looking at me and waving for me to come on over. I could not believe my luck when he asked if I would be willing to work in his store.

"I have been looking all over for a place to work," I said.

"Well, before we come to an agreement, I need to know a few things about you," he said. "Follow me."

I followed him into the store, where he told me to put my books on the end of the counter and motioned me to follow him behind the counter. A door led to a small restroom for the employees. He got down on his knees in front of the toilet, lifted the lid, took a brush and some cleanser, and started scrubbing the toilet. I mean, he really did a power scrub all around inside the bowl. When he was finished, he looked up at me. "I own this place and I can do that," he said. "Can you do that?"

"It doesn't look that difficult to me," I answered. "Yes, I can do that."

Then he took me into the back room that was long and narrow with stacks of boxes on one side and an entire wall of shelving jammed full of cans on the other side. "Here is my problem," he said. "As you can see, this is a tiny store. Nevertheless, this is an extremely busy store. Because I do not have a lot of space in the store itself, I constantly need the shelves restocked. I want you to go around the store and remember where everything is and then come out here and find out where those same items are stored. After you do that, come and let me know if you think you can do the job."

I spent some time doing as he said. As I was checking the stock on the shelves in the store room, I found some money behind some cans. I went to Webb, the owner, and asked him to come out to the store room. I showed him the money. "Someone must have mislaid this," I said.

Webb said, "You're hired."

Webb was an interesting character. He was in his late thirties, still single, and taking care of his mother. He had a small electric organ near the counter in the store and some evenings he would gather customers around and we would have sing-alongs. A couple of times a week, someone would come into the store and he would throw a head of lettuce or a tomato at them. Then it became a free-for-all, with several people joining in throwing produce at one another. It was up to me to clean up the mess. The store became busier and busier.

Webb also had a fast food stand at one end of the parking lot. It had three sides that lifted up so people could be seated around three sides of the place at a counter. He hired me to run it in the warm weather months. He had a chili recipe for hot dogs that many, many people wanted to purchase, some offering hundreds of dollars. But Webb would never sell it. He thought the place should have a name so I suggested The Dog House. He liked it, and made a huge sign that he put up on a pole out front, showing a dog halfway out of a dog house. This location was on Route 17. Many truckers, not wanting to pay the toll on the New York State Thruway, would travel this route from Buffalo to the New York City area and back. It was also a shortcut. I do believe that most of the truckers stopped at The Dog House.

Meeting so many very different people, enjoying conversations with them, and enjoying the feeling of knowing how happy they were because of the food was so much fun that I came to think it was all a great adventure rather than just a job. The Dog House became such a huge success that more people had to be hired to help serve the crowds of people in the evenings. One of our fairly regular customers was the local Roman Catholic priest. One Friday night, he was seated at the counter eating a hot dog at about eleven o'clock. One of his parishioners stopped by and sat down beside him. She noticed that he was eating a hot dog,

"Father Turner! It's Friday!" she exclaimed. "You are eating meat!"

He reached down to his watch, turned the knob, showed her his watch, "Look, it's three after midnight," he said. "Everything is O.K."

She looked at me and shrugged. I stored the incident away in my memory. It has played itself back many times as I think on certain church regulations and where they really fit in compared to Christ's teachings. Perhaps it is important to know when to turn the time to a more appropriate setting and realize that many situations really are O.K.

One day while I was busy lifting the sides of The Dog House to open for business, a large, fancy, black car drove up. When the man got out, I recognized him as the father of one of my classmates, a lawyer and a devout Roman Catholic. He walked up to me just as I finished fastening the side up.

"I have heard that you want to become a clergyman," he said.

"Yes, I feel that God has called me to be a pastor," I replied.

"That is a very high and important calling," he said. "I want you to know that in your years of education that lie ahead, if you have need of any money, the amount doesn't matter, give me a call. However, you must never tell anyone about this as long as I live. If you do, I will deny the whole thing. Here is my card; I expect a call sometime. God be with you." And he left.

In my second year working for Webb, I was restocking the cold beverage case in the store around midnight one night. He came over and told me that all the stores in the area were beginning to sell beer, so he was going to do the same or he would lose business.

"It's your store, but the minute beer comes in, I go out," I said. "I will not work in a place that sells that stuff."

"Yes, it is my store," he answered. "Just where do you think you are going to get another job?"

"I don't have a clue," I replied. "I just know I can't work in a place that sells alcoholic drinks."

"You are the best worker I have ever had; I don't want to lose you," he said. "But I do have to compete with the other stores."

I answered, "You already have them beaten just by the way you do business. Who has song fests, food riots, and constant joking with the customers the way you do?"

No more was said about the matter, but he never sold alcoholic beverages. Before I went to college, Webb, too, told me to call him if I ever needed financial help. He also told me that if I changed my mind about becoming a clergyman, he would like to take me on as a full partner in his business. While I was in college, he tore down his small store and built the largest store in the whole territory, complete with a full service butcher shop and a larger organ.

I would work from after school until around midnight and then walk the mile or so home. One night when I came into the house from work, I saw a terrible scene. The sadist had Lois bent over backwards over the kitchen sink with a butcher knife to her throat and blood running down her neck and into the sink. I grabbed a large, heavy glass ashtray and raised it over my head.

"Drop the knife or I will kill you on the spot," I yelled.

He dropped the knife and said "I think it is time for you to leave."

"That is the first thing you have ever said with which I agree," I responded. I packed my belongings in a pillowcase and walked to town, to my pastor's house. It was well after 1 o'clock in the morning. I lived there until I graduated from high school.

Although well over half a century has passed now, and I have met many remarkable, loving, fathers, every time I pray the Lord's Prayer, saying "Our Father," feelings of terror and discomfort still fill me. Early experiences leave lasting results. My experience of being mistreated and unable to do anything about it at the time left me with a strong conviction to fight the oppression of others. Understanding rather than condemning became my life's goal. My experience had great impact on how I view everything! Those experiences meld in a unique way with Christ's teachings against condemnation and the judging of others. One gives support to the other.

In the fall of 1953, I became a student at Ohio Wesleyan University. Two courses were especially helpful: Bible and debate. I had a tough time with the Bible professor because she was far more liberal than I. Nevertheless, as I look back, I certainly needed her perspective to awaken me to a deeper understanding of scripture. And the debate course has guided me in numerous debates on college campuses, public meetings, and over the radio many times since.

Going to Ohio Wesleyan opened the door to a whole new world for me. Not only did the professors prod me into much deeper thinking, I was able to have conversations with Eleanor Roosevelt, Norman Vincent Peal, Robert Frost, Charles Laughton, and Eileen Farrell. I spent an entire evening on one end of a piano bench in our fraternity house with

Duke Ellington. And, just as valuable as any of the above, I met some great students from around the world. One of my jobs on campus was operating the dishwasher after meals in Stuyvesant Hall, a female dormitory. The fellow who worked with me was Chinese and claimed to be an atheist. Practically every time we washed dishes he was compelled to recite:

"Out of the night that covers me,

Black as the pit from pole to pole,

I thank whatever gods may be,

For my unconquerable soul.

In the fell clutch of circumstance,

I have winced but not cried aloud.

Under the bludgeonings of chance,

My head is bloodied but unbowed.

Beyond this place of wrath and tears,

Looms but the horror of the shade.

And yet the menace of the years,

Finds, and shall find me, unafraid.

It matters not how strait the gate,

How charged with punishments the scroll,

I am the master of my fate,

I am the captain of my soul."

This, of course is "Invictus," by William Earnest Henley.

In my dorm were others I will never forget: a Buddhist from Burma, who was one of the kindest, most gentle, unassuming people I have ever known. I have seen few Christians who can match his caring attitude. I met a Shintoist from Japan whose father was the Japanese general who fought my Buddhist friend's father, who was a general in the Burmese army during the Second World War. There was a Jewish fellow from Brooklyn, New York, whose parents asked me to walk him to class to make sure he got there every day. Joel had a mind that I would not have believed possible if I had not watched him study. He would read a 300-page book in about 10 minutes by slowly turning the pages about two seconds at a time. One could ask him any question about anything in the book and he would not only give you the answer, he would tell you what page it was on and where it was located on the page. All of his tests were perfectly answered but he was failing because he could not be bothered with homework, writing papers, or attending classes.

Even though I had a couple of jobs on campus, I barely made it through the first year financially. In fact, toward the end of the college year, I spent a week in the infirmary because of malnutrition. I could not afford to go back the next year. I kept thinking about the financial offers from the lawyer and Webb, but something inside me would not let me call them. Ever since my mother died, I had felt alone. I came to believe that it was me against the world. Perhaps my Chinese friend's recitation of "Invictus" three times a day for a year had finally penetrated me to my depths. Whatever the reason, I could not, would not ask for help.

September 1954 found me at our Methodist college in Kansas City, Missouri, National College for Christian Workers. It was one of the two colleges in this country sponsored by the Women's Division of the Methodist Church. It is now St. Paul's School of Theology.

Around midnight one night during the first two weeks there, I finished preparing for the next day's classes and felt very hungry. I went to the room next door in the dormitory to see if my friend Sonny was still up and if he would go with me to the diner across the street. He was up, but when I asked him about going over to eat he replied, "I can't."

"Why not?" I asked.

"Look at me," he retorted.

"And what am I supposed to see?"

"I'm Negro!" he blurted out.

"So what?" I responded.

Then Sonny told me that that diner was segregated and he, as a colored person, could not eat there.

Ignorant me came back with, "That can't be. Come on, let's go."

"All right," he replied. "It's time you learned a thing or two. Let's go."

I opened the door to Mel's Diner and as we started through the door, there came a bellow from behind the counter. "Stop right there!" Everyone in the diner was staring at us. I looked over and the man was looking right at us. Then he shouted, as he pointed at me, "You can come in, but he has to stay out."

"He is my friend, not my dog," I said.

"Then you stay out, too," the man yelled.

"Not only will I stay out, so will every person on that campus across the street," I said. We left.

The next morning, I asked for a meeting of the faculty and Student Council. At the meeting, I related what had happened and that I felt that we were a Christian family and that when one of us is insulted, we are all insulted. We should boycott Mel's Diner. Unanimously, the council agreed to the boycott and to notify all on campus. We students ate our meals all at the same time in one large room. At the next meal, the student body heard the story and the resulting decision of the council. Everyone clapped and agreed.

This college had a great work opportunity program. I had several jobs on campus to help pay my way; one of them was as switchboard operator several hours a week. One evening, some three weeks after the diner event, Mel called while I was on duty. He wanted to know whom he could talk to about a problem he was having.

"What kind of a problem?" I asked.

He related that, for some reason, he was not getting any business from the college anymore and he wondered why. I told him that I could answer his question. "You kicked me and my friend out of your restaurant, and when you did that, you kicked everyone over here out of your place of business," I said.

"When did I do that?" he said. I related the incident to him and he replied, "I didn't kick you out, I kicked the 'nigger' out."

"Exactly," I replied. "You see, we are all 'niggers' over here. We are all Christians and brothers and sisters of one another."

"Oh, that is the way it is?" Mel responded. He was silent for a time and then he said, "Well, I am going under financially the way it is, so, there is nothing to lose. Let them all know they are welcome." Mel's Diner was integrated in September 1954.

In October, six of us, including Sonny, went to the movie theater up the street and the manager came out and stopped us from going in. I won't go into all the details, but we integrated the theater that very night.

I served as pastor of two churches north of Kansas City while I was in college. At the beginning of November, a man who was considered a pillar of one of the churches asked me if there was someone at college who could come out to their Christmas Eve service to sing a special song. Now, I had been told that both the communities where I served churches had "blue laws" on their town books. One of those laws stated something like, "Any nigger caught in town after sundown and before sunup can be shot." I never had this verified, but I did believe it. All this was in the back of my mind as I pondered the question concerning a vocalist for Christmas Eve, because it happened that Sonny had a beautiful voice.

I thought and prayed about the matter for several days and concluded that I would take the chance but that it was really up to Sonny. I went into Sonny's room and related the request and the situation to him and asked him if he would come out and sing at the service. He looked at me and said "Corp, you are trying to get me killed."

"I do not know if this 'blue law' thing is true or not."

"Oh, I know for a fact that such laws exist," he said. "You must take this very seriously."

"Well, I hope you will think and pray about it," I replied. "I think the blue law thing may be true and if it is, I would likely be killed right along with you. But I believe it is important enough to take a stand. Still, I can't and won't speak for you." I left Sonny to his thoughts.

About a week later, Sonny came into my room and said, "Let's do it."

I told them at church that I had found a very good soloist for the service and the word spread like wildfire. When I was appointed to these two churches, the district superintendant had made arrangements that the churches would take turns providing dinners for me since all the pastoral work (except for emergencies) had to be done on the weekend. It happened that the next Sunday I was to eat at the home of a family in this church. They lived on a farm way out in the country and had two young sons. The wife was very active in the church but her husband had never been into a church and had sworn that he never would. He was the type of man, though, who was very thoughtful, kind, and helpful. One could not help liking him.

At dinner, I told the family that I had a problem and that I needed their advice. "What is it?" the husband asked. I told them that it was very confidential and that what we talked about could not be told to anyone.

"This is getting better all the time!" he responded. "You don't have to worry about us. If these two boys say anything, I'll have their hides nailed to the barn door." With that said, I told them about the request for a singer for the Christmas Eve service.

"Oh, everyone knows about that!" the wife remarked.

I went on to say that I had found a very good singer but that he was a Negro. The man jumped up, hit his fist on the table and exclaimed, "Hot diggity, I am going to church!" Then he sat down and got very serious. "You know, don't you, that this is no joke," he said. "You could both get yourselves killed."

Then I told them about another problem I had. I needed a place to stay that night because I wanted to get an early start to go back east for Christmas.

"That's no problem," he said. "Stay here."

"But what about Sonny?" I asked. "He is going back East with me."

"He can stay here too, but he'll have to sleep with you," the husband said. "There is no other bed."

"I have been sleeping double all my life until I got to college," I answered.

The day before Christmas inevitably came. I had decided that we would drive out to the church during daylight and get there before anyone else so Sonny could hide in the church until it was time to step out and sing. When we got close to the village, Sonny climbed into the back seat and lay down so he could not be seen. I drove to the back of the church and took him in through a back door and into a storage room behind the pulpit to wait. The pianist, Elaine, was also a good friend of mine from college, so she was in on what was happening. As people filed into the church I could hear them whisper to one another.

"I don't see anybody new, do you?"

"I don't think he was able to get anyone."

I started the service and when it was time for Sonny to sing, Elaine started the introduction to "O Holy Night." Sonny stepped out and there was one huge intake of breath that sounded like every bit of air was sucked out of the room. Sonny began to sing. When he finished, he went on to sing "I Wonder as I Wander." Practically everyone was crying, including me.

After the service, I thought we would never get out of there. It seemed like every single person wanted to at least grab his hand if not squeeze him half to death. They fell in love with him. I believe Christmas really came that night. I also believe that my oppressive experience growing up brought me to that night.

Chapter 2

Experience Goes to Work

After college, I was appointed to two churches on the northern border of Pennsylvania while I attended seminary at a Seventh Day Baptist Seminary at Alfred University in Alfred, New York. I was very interested in working with youth, so during the first 20 years of my ministry I also did a lot of youth work. This not only involved my local churches, but I was also Sub-District and District youth director in Missouri, Washington, D.C., and Syracuse, New York. It so happens that at one of those churches in Pennsylvania, the youth had questions about sexuality concerns. This was not unique to them; it was true in every single church I served. The questions began at this church because of a house of prostitution in town. The young people seemed to know about it although the adults seemed oblivious. Shortly after this topic came up in my youth group, I was leading a Cub Scout troop in the fellowship hall of our church one evening when the town constable came in and wanted to talk to me. He had just "discovered" the existence of this house of prostitution and wanted my assistance in deciding what to do about it. He was a Baptist. I asked him why he had not gone to his own pastor about the problem. He said something to the effect that the pastor would not know anything about such things.

Apparently, my discussions with the youth and my urging them to talk to their parents had stirred up some questions with the constable. As a result of our conversation, I contacted the Baptist pastor and the Assemblies of God pastor and we met with the constable in his living room the next Friday evening. The constable happened to live on a corner opposite the house of prostitution. On that one night, we counted 52 cars from New York State parking on the street, with the men going to the house in question. It was decided that the constable would contact the state police, and he did so.

Not long after that, I had an appointment to take my car in for servicing at a garage in a nearby community. I was sitting in the waiting room until my car was ready when one of these "ladies of the night" walked into the waiting room and stood over by the water fountain. Soon a state police officer sauntered in and walked over to the water fountain.

"What do you want?" she said.

"You have to close your business for a little while," He responded, "We are going to raid your place next Friday night. Let your clients know and get rid of any evidence. You will need to find a new location." He walked out. Then, she left.

A few days later, I went into the local hardware store to buy a griddle. The owner was a member of my church and on the church's Board of Trustees. As I paid for the griddle, he said, "We try to grow this town, we get a new business, and you drive it out." Was he joking? Maybe.

I also learned while I was there that one needs to work with both the parents and the youth when dealing with sexuality issues. By the time I got my third appointment, which was my first in Syracuse, New York, and started getting these sexuality questions, I decided to get some help since I was really quite ignorant concerning the topic. I went to the only place I knew that dealt with such concerns: Planned Parenthood. One of their educators worked with me and several of the parents from my church as we developed an eight-week course on sex education. When it was finished, both the parents and the youth declared that it was the best thing the church had ever done.

As just noted, my journey in sex education began as a result of questions that came up in my youth groups in the late 1950s. In all of my churches, youth had sexuality questions and issues. I heard that the Unitarian Universalist Church had developed a sex education curriculum, so I contacted them. They allowed me to go through their leadership training program and use their curriculum. I had to adapt it because some of the material was far too explicit to be acceptable to many of our parents.

Fortunately, Dr. Courtoy of our Youth Division in Nashville, Tennessee, developed a sexuality curriculum for our denomination a few years later. He held education seminars to certify adults to use the curriculum. I was fortunate enough to be one of those and was consecrated by my Annual Conference to be an approved sex educator. Later, I shared in further developing the United Methodist curriculum.

One Sunday in the 1970s, right after a worship service, a young woman came up to me very distraught and said she wanted to talk to me privately. We went to my office and she burst out crying. She related that the night before, her 16-year-old nephew had been beaten practically to the point of death by his father because he had learned that his son was homosexual. Her nephew was now in the hospital. The whole family was taking sides, causing terrible splits in what had been a great extended family. Could I help?

I was stunned, chagrined, and very angry. Old feelings of what it was like to be ostracized and bullied came rushing back. To add to that, I am the type who always wants to be able to help; however, I knew absolutely nothing about this issue or what to do about it. What kind of advice could I give other than to say I would pray for all concerned? But, for me, a prayer in which you are not able to also apply yourself is only partial and practically a mockery. I did tell her that I would pray, but also responded, "I'll have to learn what I can and then see what I can do."

My life's experience up to this time, through college, through seminary, and up to the 1970s—including all the sex education training—none of this had ever brought up anything about homosexuality, nor had I ever given it a moment of thought. Nor was there any inkling about it in the Discipline of the Church.

I began filling any spare time getting books from the library, researching, and taking notes from some 100 authors on every side of the issue concerning homosexuality: professors, theologians from Baptist to Roman Catholic, psychologists, sociologists, scientists, medical professionals, and those with various theories and opinions. I also attended seminars led by several of these authors.

I gathered my newly acquired information and put it in a 40-page paper. In discussing what I was doing with some of my clergy friends, one of them warned me to be careful, saying that I could be kicked out of the ministry. With that, I decided to send a copy of my paper to the bishop. I did not want to serve under any false pretenses. A few days later, the bishop called me and applauded me for doing an outstanding job. He went on to ask me to lead workshops for the clergy in the Area. Our Area included three Conferences and some 1200 churches.

I was part of a ministerial group that met once a month for breakfast and discussed various church-related issues, and I brought up this topic at our next meeting. At the breakfast, I told them about my paper and the bishop's request and asked if they would be willing to be a core group to start the first seminar. I also suggested that we have a homosexual Christian to be present at the seminar to help us with his or her perspective of the issue. One of the clergy, whom I had considered a fairly close friend, jumped out of his chair.

"That is an oxymoron!" he screamed. "There is no such thing as a Christian being a homosexual, and furthermore, I won't be a part of your seminar!" He then stomped out of the restaurant. I ended up paying his bill.

Late one evening a few years later, I received a phone call. The man was sobbing so that at first I couldn't make out what he was saying. But I did recognize his voice, and it was the screaming clergyman. His son had just revealed to him that he was homosexual.

"Help me," he pleaded. "What shall I do?"

I could write a book of similar instances in which parents are adamantly against homosexuality only to discover later that one of their children, or more than one, is homosexual. The most recent such incident was in 2012. In spring of that year, I was invited to organize and lead the worship service at a college in New York state for a reenactment commemorating the 150th anniversary of the Civil War. I also was invited to give the final lecture for a class on the topic "The Civil War and Religion." Since I was in the area, I stopped to worship at a church where I had served from 1962-1972. I had endured an ongoing conflict with a mother in that church about the issue of homosexuality. She was absolutely convinced that one chose to be homosexual and with proper Christian teaching, no one would make such a decision. To make sure her children were not corrupted by public school teachings, she home-schooled her children. As I went into my former church, even before I could sit down, this woman came up to me and told me about her daughter's recent marriage. Her properly educated daughter had married another female. Furthermore, this mother couldn't love her daughter-in-law more.

To return to the clergy seminars the bishop asked me to lead: As a result of the seminars, my paper was copied and traveled somehow all over the country. I received calls from professors at several universities asking permission to use my paper. A whole ministry developed around dealing with sexuality issues. I found myself giving sexuality seminars in churches, schools, colleges, Rotary and Kiwanis clubs, and debating on college campuses and over the radio. I have also taught classes on human sexuality as a part of the health curriculum in junior high schools and given talks in high schools.

I continued my sex education by participating in seminars with Masters and Johnson of world renown; Drs. Beryl and Noam Chernick of Canada, and, later, attending many week-long sex education events developed by Dr. Sol Gordon of Syracuse University over several years. He organized these educational events in collaboration with the University of Massachusetts, Syracuse University, The University of Pennsylvania, The University of Virginia, and Elmira College. These educational classes were conducted by professors from the universities. I also took a graduate course at Wesley Theological Seminary on the Bible and homosexuality, taught by Dr. Phillip Wogaman.

After the Conference workshops that I led for the clergy, homosexuals started appearing at my churches for counseling and worship. I have spent the rest of my life working with homosexual people and trying to educate my denomination. The easy part is working with the individuals. I will always regret not being able to be more helpful to that original family that alerted me to this ongoing tragedy: the division among us Christians, who claim we love everybody; Christians, whom Jesus has urged to condemn no one.

It became very obvious to me that this love we talk about so easily is only an illusion. Many who call themselves Christian absolutely do not love everyone. I have learned that the common saying, "I love the sinner but not the sin," is a smokescreen, a rationalization that is almost always false. Their hatred of the sin envelops them as well as the suspected "sinner." Too often, the real feelings show through and lead to suffering or even death for the "sinner." This issue is no mere Theological or Christological game—it is life or death. Our church has chosen to become a part of this disaster. Of all the things the Scriptures list as sinful, homosexuality is not one of them. However, the Church has decided that it will list only one thing as "incompatible with Christian teaching" and that is homosexuality. Apparently lying, stealing, cheating, pride, murder, etc., are not incompatible, but homosexuality, which was never listed as such, is now "incompatible with Christian teaching." Just where did the Church get this idea? From what "Christian teaching" does it originate?

I hope that sharing my experience in these first two chapters has illustrated how my experience has colored my perspective in approaching Scripture, tradition, and reason. In my opinion, every single person should evaluate his or her own experience and note how it defines his or her perspective. Some have learned to hate. I have learned to care, to accept, and to love. My reading of Jesus' teachings reveals the same.

Chapter 3

"The Word of God"

In the first chapter, I told of my reading the Scriptures at age 13 and that a well-meaning church member had told me that the Bible is written by God, that it is unchanging, and literally true, meaning inerrant. He said that every word is from God and God does not make mistakes. In many of our churches, when the reading of the Scriptures ends during the worship service, the liturgist often says, "The Word of God for the people of God." What is meant by "the Word of God?" As we shall see, scriptural authority and meaning has changed through the ages. It was not until 1442, at the Council of Florence, that the "Doctrine of Inspiration" was adopted. Many believe that this doctrine about the Scriptures was always so, from the very beginning of Christianity. In a way, that concept has existed for a very long time in various forms, but what does it mean? What is meant by "the Word of God"? What is meant by inspiration and inerrancy? What evidence is there to support the concepts of inspiration, authority, inerrancy, and the meaning of "the Word of God"?

The Jews viewed Scripture as the "exclamation of the Holy Spirit."[1] As such, they believed it impossible for contradictions or real differences to appear in the text. However, they also believed in levels of inspiration. Although they viewed all Scripture as inspired, the Jews did not see all Scripture on an equal level of inspiration. Moses' writings were viewed as the dictation of God. However, the scholars who have studied these writings have discovered that they were written some 300 years after Moses lived. The prophets and the *Hagiographa* were seen as inspired but in a lesser degree since these books were not given by actual dictation, but only through inspiration.[2]

Hagiographa is the Hebrew term for writings. It is the third part of the Old Testament canon, the other two being the Law and the Prophets. It contains 11 books: the three books that are, in a special sense, designated as the poetic books par excellence, Job, Proverbs, and Psalms; the five Megillot ("rolls"), which are read on five different festivals and include Canticles, Ruth, Lamentations, Ecclesiastes, and Esther; and the books of Daniel, Ezra-Nehemiah (considered as two parts of one book), and Chronicles. Although theologically the Jews held a high view of Scripture, their tradition had so manipulated the text that they had, in effect, nullified its teaching. Jesus criticized them not for their belief but their unbelief.

How did the concept of inspiration of Scriptures get started? In 382, Pope Damasus I commissioned Jerome to make a revision of older Latin translations. The translation named the Vulgate was the result. By the

13th century, this revision had become the commonly used translation, and it ultimately became the definitive and officially promulgated Latin version of the Bible in the Roman Catholic Church. This translation used the word "inspiration." Inspiration comes from the Latin noun *inspiratio* and from the verb *inspirare*. Inspirare is a compound term resulting from the Latin prefix *in* (inside, into) and the verb *spirare* (to breathe). Inspirare meant originally "to blow into." In classic Roman times, inspirare had already come to mean "to breathe deeply" and assumed also the figurative sense of "to instill [something] in the heart or in the mind of someone." But here we are paying all of our attention to a Latin term rather than the original Greek term *theopneumatos*, which had a different meaning. Part of our problem is that too many rely on the Latin interpretation rather than the original Greek.

Jerome translated the Greek *theopneumatos* in 2 Timothy 3:16-17, as *divinitus inspirata*, "divinely breathed into." (In English, that passage reads: "All Scripture is given by inspiration of God [theopneumatos], and is profitable for doctrine, for reproof, for correction, for instruction in righteousness: that the man of God may be perfect, thoroughly furnished unto all good works.") While theopneumatos is rendered in the Vulgate as the Latin divinitus inspirata ("divinely breathed into"), some modern English translations opt for "God-breathed" (NIV) or "breathed out by God" (ESV) and avoid the word inspiration altogether, since its connotation, unlike its Latin root, leans toward breathing in instead of breathing out. The word *pneu* in Greek and *pneuma* means variously breeze, wind, breath, and spirit.

When Jesus conversed with the Samaritan woman at Jacob's well,[3] she brought up the big difference between the Jews and the Samaritans regarding the place where worship should take place. The Samaritans believed God had told them to build a Temple on Mt. Gerizeim.[4] After all, this area had been the area of the Patriarchs and Shechem was one of the most sacred sites in all Israel. Joshua had made the new covenant there on arrival from Egypt. The giving of manna had stopped and the first Passover in the Holy Land was celebrated there. Centuries later, the Jews had built a temple on the mountain in Jerusalem. In response to the comment of the woman at the well, Jesus taught that the time is near when all would worship God in *pneumati*, meaning "in spirit and in truth." There is nothing here to imply dictation, doctrine, inerrancy, or even words in the use of the word pneu, or pneumati. It was a spiritual relationship with God.

What do the Scriptures reveal? In our early religious history, the gods, and even Yahweh, were perceived as anthropomorphic. In Genesis 32:24-30, Jacob wrestles with a man whom he later discovers is El. In Exodus 3, at the "Burning Bush" Theophany, Moses asks for God's name because he knows that when he gets back to Egypt, the people will want to know the name of this God who is freeing them. After all, they know about many gods. Different gods with different attributes had different names. When people changed, their names changed. Abram became Abraham, Jacob became Israel, Esau became Edom, Saul became Paul.[5] One sees again and again throughout the Scriptures the uniqueness in names for God. All this emphasizes that the other names used for various gods in the Old Testament were NOT just old names for Yahweh. However, this becomes confusing because of what the very late writers, the Priestly writers, have done. After the 587 exile to Babylon, they attempted to revise or expand scriptural history by adding to many of the writings. In Exodus 6:2-3, they wrote, "Elohim also spoke to Moses and said to him, I am Yahweh, I appeared to Abraham, Isaac, and Jacob as Elohim El Shaddai; but by my name Yahweh, I did not make myself known." Joshua 24:2, however, makes it very clear: "Thus says Yahweh, the Elohim of Israel: long ago your ancestors—Terah and his sons Abraham and Nahor—lived beyond the Euphrates and served other gods." Names were very significant. The incarnation of God in Jesus meant that Jesus was to reveal the very nature, the way of God.

Exodus 33:11 states that Moses was allowed to see God's face. Yet verse 20 states that Moses cannot see God's face for no man can see God's face and live. Then, in verse 23, Moses was allowed to see God's back as he walked away. But the prophets, in Isaiah 40:18-26, stated that God did not have a body, was not anthropomorphic; rather, God was a universal, spiritual being, not physical, so one cannot make an image or idol.

In Judaic and Christian usage, *pneuma* is a common word for "spirit" as in the Septuagint and the Greek New Testament. In John 3:5, for example, pneuma is the Greek word translated into English as spirit: "Verily, verily, I say unto thee, except a man be born of water and of the Spirit (pneuma), he cannot enter into the kingdom of God."

Furthermore, the church fathers often referred to writings other than the documents that formed or would form the biblical canon as "inspired,"[6] and they believed editors of the Bible were led or influenced by God, with the result that their writings may be designated in some sense the "Word of God."[7] Those definitions are very different from the "Doctrine of Inspiration."

Although Jerome's translation of the Vulgate is faulty, the Roman Catholic Church holds the Bible as inspired by God, but does not view God as the direct author of the Bible, in the sense that He does not put a ready-made book in the mind of the inspired person.[8] As summarized by Karl Keating,[9] the authors of the Roman Catholic apologetic for the inspiration of Scripture first consider the Scriptures as a merely historical source, and then attempt to derive the divinity of Jesus from the information contained therein, illuminated by the tradition of the Catholic Church and by what they consider to be common knowledge about human nature. After offering evidence that Jesus is indeed God, the authors argue that Jesus' biblical promise to establish a church that will never perish cannot be empty, and that promise, they believe, implies an infallible teaching authority vested in the church. They conclude that this authoritative church teaches that the Bible's own doctrine of inspiration is in fact the correct one.

In the Protestant churches, we have an evangelical perspective, a biblical inerrancy view, a neo-orthodox view, a modernist Christian view, etc. Evangelicals view the Bible as a genuinely human product, but one whose creation was superintended by the Holy Spirit, preserving the authors' works from error without eliminating their specific concerns, situation, or style. This divine involvement, they say, allowed the biblical writers to communicate without corrupting God's own message both to the immediate recipients of the writings and to those who would come after. Some evangelicals have labeled the conservative or traditional view as "verbal, plenary inspiration of the original manuscripts," by which they mean that each word (not just the overarching ideas or concepts) was meaningfully chosen under the superintendence of God. Evangelicals acknowledge textual variations between biblical accounts of apparently identical events and speeches. These are seen as complementary, not contradictory, and are explained as the differing viewpoints of different authors. For instance, the Gospel of Matthew was intended to communicate the Gospel to Jews, the Gospel of Luke to Greeks, and the Gospel of Mark to Romans. Evangelical apologists such as John W. Haley in his book, "Alleged Discrepancies in the Bible," and Norman Geisler in "When Critics Ask," have proposed answers to hundreds of claimed contradictions. Some discrepancies are accounted for by changes from the *autographa* (the original manuscripts) that have been introduced in the copying process, either deliberately or accidentally.

Many evangelicals consider biblical inerrancy and/or biblical infallibility to be the necessary consequence of the Bible's doctrine of inspiration (see, for example, the Westminster Confession of Faith or the Chicago Statement on Biblical Inerrancy). Note that none of this rationale comes from the Scriptures themselves.

Three basic approaches to "inspiration" are often described when the evangelical approach to Scripture is discussed.[10]

1. Dictation Theory: God dictated the books of the Bible word by word as if the biblical authors were dictating machines.[11]

2. Verbal Plenary Inspiration: This view gives a greater role to the human writers of the Bible, while maintaining a belief that God

preserved the integrity of the words of the Bible. "The effect of inspiration was to move the authors so as to produce the words God wanted."[12] In this view the human writers' "individual backgrounds, personal traits, and literary styles were authentically theirs, but had been providentially prepared by God for use as his instrument in producing Scripture."[13]

3. Dynamic Inspiration: The thoughts contained in the Bible are inspired, but the words used were left to the individual writers.[14] Nevertheless, according to T.D. Lea and H.P. Griffen, "no respected evangelicals maintain that God dictated the words of Scripture."[15]

The evangelical position has been criticized as being circular both by non-Christians and by Christians such as Catholic and Orthodox authors, who accept the doctrine but reject the Protestant arguments in favor of it. These critics claim that the Bible can only be used to prove doctrines of biblical inspiration if the doctrine is assumed to begin with.[16]

The view shared by Modernist (liberal Christianity) and progressive Christianity typically rejects the idea that the Bible is divinely inspired in a unique way. Some advocates of higher criticism who espouse this view even go so far as to regard the Bible as purely a product of human invention. However, most form critics, such as Rudolf Bultmann and Walter Brueggemann, still regard the Bible as a sacred text, just not a text that communicates the unaltered word of God. They see it instead as true, divinely inspired theology mixed with foreign elements that can sometimes be inconsistent with the overarching messages found in Scripture and that have discernible roots in history, mythology, or ancient cultural/cultic practices. As such, form critics attempt to separate the kernel of inspired truth from the husk that contains it, doing so through various exegetical methods.

The neo-orthodox doctrine of inspiration is summarized by saying that the Bible is the Word of God but not the words of God. Only when one reads the text does it become the Word of God to the reader. This view is a reaction to the Modernist doctrine, which, neo-orthodox proponents argue, eroded the value and significance of the Christian faith, and simultaneously a rejection of the idea of textual inerrancy. Karl Barth and Emil Brunner were primary advocates of this approach.

Biblical inerrancy is the doctrine that the Bible, in its original manuscripts, is accurate and totally free from error of any kind, that "Scripture in the original manuscripts does not affirm anything that is contrary to fact."[17] Some equate inerrancy with infallibility; others do not.[18] The trouble is that such a distinction is nowhere to be found in Jesus' own teaching. Such thinking seems to be precluded by testimony both to the unqualified historical accuracy and the inspiration of the Old Testament. The attempt to discriminate seems to be a product of the 19th and 20th centuries. The official statement in favor of biblical inerrancy is proclaimed to be the Chicago Statement on Biblical Inerrancy, which was published in the *Journal of the Evangelical Theological Society* in 1978. The signatories to the Chicago Statement on Biblical Inerrancy affirm that, since there are no extant original manuscripts of the Bible, those that exist cannot be considered inerrant. The signatories also affirm, however, that the existing manuscripts are faithful copies of the original manuscripts. But how can one know this when one has never seen the original?

A minority of biblical inerrantists go further than the official statement on biblical inerrancy, arguing that the original text has been perfectly preserved and passed down through time; this is absolutely false concerning most of the Old Testament writings. The original language texts that are used by modern translators as the source for translations of the Bible are reconstructions of the original text, which are based upon scholarly comparison of thousands of biblical manuscripts (such as the Dead Sea Scrolls) and thousands of biblical citations in the writings of the early church fathers.

Then came the "Doctrine of Inerrancy." What does that mean? Some assume that everyone means the same thing by these terms. The above shows clearly that we do not. And, a bigger problem: how do we justify the Old Testament laws with the Gospel of Jesus? The different ways of approaching Scripture as God's Word results in some "Christians" telling other "Christians" that they are going to hell! No judgment there!

What is the basic difference? All agree that the Scriptures are "the Word of God" and that the writers were "inspired." But, as discussed above, there are very different ideas about what is meant by both of these terms. Physically speaking, inspire means to breathe in. Mentally, inspired means to be stimulated or influenced, to be motivated. It does not mean to be controlled or dictated to. And, as also noted above, those are not the true meaning of theopneumatos. The Bible is a collection of writings that reveals the writer's understandings of God relating to various life circumstances. As we shall see, those understandings develop and change. This not only does not demand the acceptance of any arbitrary doctrine of inspiration, in fact, it works against such an idea.

The Bible writers were influenced to write just as we are influenced by God when we read what they wrote. Both inspiration and inerrancy as doctrines are false doctrines if, on the one hand, inspiration means God somehow dictated the Scriptures while on the other, if God gave them, they cannot contain any mistakes. To claim that the Scriptures are literally transpired by God is the worst kind of blasphemy. It claims that finite man is able to perfectly understand the infinite mind of God.[19] There is proof in Scriptures again and again that this certainly is not so; I provide examples at the end of this chapter. This type of belief leads to textproofing—taking Scripture from one place and using it for one's own purposes somewhere else. The doctrine of literal inspiration is just a theory that has resulted in many aberrations of the Christian faith, such as the flat earth society, the killing of witches, the institution of slavery, holy wars, the Crusades, burning heretics at the stake, the Civil War, the Ku Klux Klan, and World War II, to give just a few examples.

Jesus condemned this practice. The Scribes and Pharisees were constantly looking for ways to discredit Jesus. For example, they observed the disciples eating without washing their hands and they told Jesus he was breaking the law, or the elders' tradition. Jesus called them hypocrites and quoted Isaiah to them: "The people honor me with their lips but their heart is far from me. In vain do you worship me, teaching human precepts as doctrines. You abandon the Commandment of God and hold to human tradition." Then Jesus used the commandment to honor your father and mother as an example, saying: "They excuse some from this Commandment by saying they do not have to give money they owe to their parents if they claim it is a gift to God. God has priority, thus they find a way out from honoring the Commandment." Then Jesus gathered the people for a teaching moment, declaring that it is "not what goes into one that defiles one, rather, what comes out."[20]

Those who believe the Scriptures are the Word of God because God dictated them in one way or another have not truly studied the Bible, nor do they know how we came to have the Bible. Others understand that, while many stories reveal eternal truths, they are not literally true in detail; and, furthermore, many mistakes or disagreements do occur. These people also see God revealed in the development of beliefs and the change in cultural relationships. The Scriptures within themselves show great change as concepts develop; I will illustrate this later in this book.

The one side believes that everything we need to know is in the Scriptures, making them another god. If this were true, there would be no need of God beyond the Bible itself. If that is so, the need for God in our lives today is a moot point. Others believe that God is just as real and revelatory today as ever. Some would say those on the one side are literalists and those on the other are liberals. But let me confuse you more. I, for example, am as literal as one can be on some portions of the Bible, while on others I am as liberal as one can be. There are literalists, letteralists, and liberals. Usually the same person is all three, but on different issues for different reasons, at different times.

Note the changing concepts in Scripture: The early religious believed that God was anthropomorphic; that god, or God, had a face, a back, arms, could walk and talk. The prophets began to grow beyond this kind of thinking and Jesus taught that God is Spirit. There was polytheism for more than 1000 years, then monolateralism (one God among many gods), and finally, monotheism. Moses believed rules could provide righteous living. The Scriptures themselves tell us that the Ten Commandments were given at four different places: Mt. Hebron, Mt. Moab, Kadesh, and Mt. Sinai. Some texts tell us Moses wrote down the Commandments and some tell us that God wrote them down. Joshua, upon coming back to Canaan, started a 100-years war trying to eliminate those who believed differently.

Jesus taught that what makes a difference is what is on the inside. Love comes from the inside, as opposed to legalism, which comes from outside. Some believe in personal salvation, which can result in a self-centered spiritual development, rejecting what are considered worldly situations. Others understand that salvation leads them to center on others and to relieve world problems. Each has a different concept of the Word of God.

What one believes about God is life changing and action changing. We can center on law, and thus on condemnation, or we can follow Christ, who taught that love, not condemnation, was God's way. Jesus taught that we must be a good neighbor to all. Each of us needs to explore what "the Word of God" really means.

The proof that God did not tell the writers what to write is in the fact that God would have known certain facts and would not have made certain mistakes. Nor would the God that Jesus revealed have included centuries of practices such as polytheism, fertility cult worship, and polygamy in his holy word. God would know how he created this world and, therefore, would not have given two completely different stories of creation. God would know the location where he gave something as important as the Ten Commandments. God would not have us taking on the Persian pagan God of evil, Satan, as a part of a monotheistic faith.

So, what is the Bible? How did we get it?

Chapter 4

Biblical Background

Let us start with a few questions. Do you believe our God would include fertility cult worship in his revelation of the way he created things to be? Do you believe our God would accept fertility cult gods for more than 1000 years of our religious history? Do you believe in polytheism? Why would the one and only God have us worshipping many gods for some thousand years if he were a jealous God having no other gods before him? If God is jealous of being the only God, why did he include in the Ten Commandments (Exodus 20:1f), "then Elohim spoke all these words, I am the Yahweh, your Elohim who brought you out of the Land of Egypt, out of the house of slavery; you shall have no other gods before me." *Elohim* is plural for the many seasonal and storm gods who are listed in many of the pagan writings found all the way from Sumaria up the Euphrates and down to Ugarit and worshipped by the Patriarchs. What does it mean—again, within the Ten Commandments themselves—in Exodus 20:5 where God says of other gods and idols,

"You shall not bow down to them or worship them, for I the Yahweh, your Elohim, am a jealous Elohim"? It is very evident that God would not have put it this way, again, including pagan fertility cult gods. Why, in the Ten Commandments, is God both a monotheistic God and polytheistic fertility cult gods? These stories are the amalgamation of different traditions brought together by some redactor.

If you have read the preface to your Bible, you came across some very important information concerning the different spellings LORD, Lord, GOD, and God. The words in all capitals refer to Yahweh. "God" means Elohim and "Lord" means Adonai, and those were fertility cult gods. If you pay attention to these spellings, plus the many other names for gods, you will soon realize that the first thousand years or so of biblical history is all about fertility cult worship and rituals, polytheism. If it was God who gave us the Scriptures and was jealous about any other gods, would he have included other gods in the text? Of course not!

And while we are considering the Ten Commandments, why does God not know where he gave them? Moses received them, so he should know. What do the Scriptures tell us? I will discuss more about the writers later, but the Deuteronomist (or "D") writers have the Ten Commandments given at Mt. Horeb in Deuteronomy 4:9-19; 5:1-5; and 16:21-27, and the same school of writers also claim the commandments were given at Moab in Deut. 12-28 and Deut. 29. The Priestly writers have them given at Mt. Sinai in Exodus 19:1-2, 24:15-18, 34:15-35, and 40:34-38; but also at Kadesh in Numbers 15 and 18-19; and at Moab in Numbers 29-30 and 35-36. So the Scriptures themselves tell us that the Ten Commandments were given at four different places. Furthermore, sometimes the Scriptures say that the Commandments are written down by God and sometimes by Moses.[21] What, then, is the answer? Where were they given? Who actually wrote them down? Because of the contradictions in the Scriptures, we will never know. There are many other examples but this is enough to illustrate the point. We need to be very careful about how we use the doctrine of literalism and inerrancy.

Another problem we face has to do with whether the Old Testament and New Testament have equal authority. If they are both given by God, they must have equal authority. But if we go by the true meaning of the writers, as opposed to the Doctrine of Inspiration, we have an entirely different situation. We now can read them in connection with man's search to understand God, as opposed to the Scriptures being dictated by God. If we read the Old Testament laws as being from God, laws that ended up judging and condemning everyone, how could the New Testament, where Jesus taught that neither he nor his followers were to judge or condemn anyone, be from the same God? It was not that the texts were from God, but from writers trying to understand God and how God works through us.

Also, many of the stories in the Bible are told not to be taken literally but rather to teach an important truth. That truth, or revelation, is couched in a memorable story. The story is only a tool to present the truth, as the following examples show.

Genesis 2:4-25 is the original story of Creation as far as our Scriptures are concerned. Note that in this version, both "LORD" and "God" are used—both Yahweh and Elohim. Note, also, the order of creation. In this story, man was created before plants or animals—before there was anything to eat! Woman was created last and from man's rib, and woman was created for companionship. This story was written around 850 BC.

However, in Genesis 1-2:5, we see that God (Elohim) is named in a form that is plural for the fertility cult gods. This is used throughout this story along with the plural "us" and "our," indicating polytheism all through the story. Genesis 1:26, 27 states, "Let us make humankind in our image...So Elohim created humankind in his image."

Although Genesis 1f. (f means "and following") is one of the latest writings, it appears first and is steeped in polytheism. It appears first because it is about creation, not because of its written chronology. It claims we are made in Elohim's image, or likeness. The word "image" is equally defined as "likeness," thus both terms are used in the various translations. While image conjures up ideas about what Elohim looks like, likeness has more to do with attributes, behavior. The word *Adam*, a Euphemism for mankind, is used. Although Adam is personified, the word really means mankind—that is what makes it an eponym, just as Eve is an eponym for womankind. The creation stories are at the beginning of the Scriptures because they are about the beginning, not because they were written first. The story that appears first was actually completed after the exile to Babylon in 589-87 BC. It was written in a seven day format to emphasize the importance of keeping the Sabbath on the seventh day, not to tell how creation literally came about. In point of fact, the story itself ends with telling us that creation took generations: "These are the generations of the heaven and the earth when they were created" (Genesis 2:4a). This polytheistic story, of course, presents the creation of humankind for the purpose of procreation. Procreation was the big concern for the fertility cult religions. We have noted that the original creation story was written some 500 years earlier, and it emphasized companionship. Procreation is not mentioned at all in the original story.

Although Genesis 1f. was rewritten by the Priestly writers around 500 BC to emphasize the importance of the Sabbath (again, more about the writers later), it includes the term Elohim, which comes from around 700 BC. Therefore, the story must have been constructed on a much older story. Consider being created in God's likeness. To be like another is to behave like another. And I believe people do behave the way they believe God is. Here is another part of our problem: we say we believe in one God, yet different people give God different attributes. And this problem is revealed repeatedly all through the Old Testament Scriptures. The Scriptures refer to God with different names; those different names carry different attributes at different times; pagan polytheism is mixed with monotheism, as in this story; and fertility cult gods are included with the God of Israel. Without careful reading, it is easy to assume that Scripture is referring to the same God all the time and we therefore get confused about the attributes we are assigning to God. I have even heard the song "El Shaddai" sung in churches. In fact, it is included in our hymnal:

> El Shaddai, El Shaddai,
>
> El-Elyon na Adonai,
>
> Age to age you're still the same,
>
> By the power of the name.

El Shaddai, El Shaddai,

Erkahmka na Adonai,

I will praise you 'til I die,

El Shaddai.

This song implies that all four gods named are merely different names for the same God, Yahweh. The fact is, they are four different fertility cult gods with different attributes. They had nothing to do with the monotheistic God, Yahweh. El Shaddai, for example, was the pagan god of violent destruction who is named in many of the pagan religious tablets that have been unearthed. The Patriarchs would say that he went up the east coast of North America in late October 2012, when we called him Hurricane Sandy.

Observe in the Genesis 1 story that the order of creation has both man and woman created last. Furthermore, the purpose for creating males and females is procreation. That fits perfectly with using Elohim and "us" and "our," because that is basically what the fertility cults were all about: fertility and procreation of people, animals, and crops. If God gave these stories, why did the one and only God include fertility cult gods as our creators? Why did God not know how he created? The order of creation is entirely different in the two different stories. Perhaps one of the biggest divisive issues among those calling themselves Christians through the last hundred years or so has been the disagreement concerning how creation took place. On the basis of one of the stories we have "creationism" or "divine design" at war with the theory of evolution, and this totally neglects the other story, ignoring the fact that the two stories present totally different orders of creation. Why two very different stories of creation? Were the collators of the writings stupid when they chose to put these two obviously very different stories side by side? Is one correct and the other wrong?

Obviously, these stories were not meant to be used the way they are misused by many today. They are faith stories with a very important truth. They were NOT intended to explain HOW creation came about, but to present the fact that, however God chose to create, God did it. It may be this way, it may be that way, it may be another way. God did it. But because many do not know what the Bible is or its history, nor how to read it, we have this great divisive issue in the church today.

The original story emphasizes companionship. The much later story (by about 500 years) emphasizes procreation. Many outspoken leaders in the faith, including those in the Roman Catholic Church, have constructed dogma based on the later story, totally neglecting the original story to the extent that the original seems never to have existed at all. And, because of Augustine's theory of the fall of man and the notion of original sin, the resulting dogmas have become the root of many of our issues concerning sexuality to this day; especially those based on misuse of sperm. All these dogmas had nothing to do with what the Scriptures really have to say.

Let's look at another story, Noah and the flood (a story, by the way, for which there is no place in biblical history). With the rains coming, do you really believe that Noah had time to build that huge ship, go to the arctic and bring back two polar bears, to Siberia to get a couple of yaks, to India for two elephants, to China to get a pair of panda bears, to Florida for two alligators, to the Antarctic for a couple of imperial penguins, and all the rest? If that really, literally happened, I want to meet up with Noah some day and tell him what I think about his rescuing those two pesky mosquitoes!

Again, we get hung up on the details when the point in this story is the rainbow as a way of reminding us of the teaching that God will not destroy us again because of our misbehavior, no matter how upset he gets with us.

Conversely, those dynamics that are left out in one's reading can be a great handicap as well. The true knowledge of a text does not come simply from the print on the page. The words printed there come out of a history that may go back thousands of years, including a conglomeration of very different understandings, customs, and religious experiences of the writers. The more one knows of the origin of the particular writing, the better one can understand its purpose. For example, almost all of the laws and customs of the Old Testament are not unique to Judaism.[22] They are very similar to the pagan customs and most of the laws adopted by the Semetic Tribes of the Nuzi and Mani texts of Mesopotamia in 2800-1760 BC and of the Hammurrabi Code of 1780 BC—all of which were pagan cults! Basically, the only laws that are different are those against pagan rituals and against worshipping other gods. Why would a God who is jealous of the idea of other gods choose the laws of pagan worshippers for the Jews to follow? He would not! It was not God, it was the writers.

If God is the same eternally, and God is the only God and a jealous God, and God gave us the Scriptures, why was there such a drastic change in some of the concepts in the Bible? For example, all the

Patriarchs believed in polytheism and worshiped fertility cult gods and goddesses for some thousand years. Polygamy endured for even longer than that, as did the use of concubines. The Patriarchs had at least two wives with some having many more. Solomon had 700 wives and 300 concubines.

For centuries, one was to marry within the family to keep the blood line pure, for that is how one lived on after death, they believed, in one's descendants. Abraham married his sister; Isaac and Jacob married their cousins. Jacob not only married cousins, he married sisters. Adultery was wrong because the blood lines were not to be adulterated.

It is also important to keep in mind that the first 1000 years of biblical history were passed on by word of mouth and were not written down until after 950 BC. How far back could oral history go? Bishop Ushur, who died in 1646, formulated a timeline of biblical events by researching stories in the Bible. As a result, he claimed that creation took place in 4004 BC. Many Christians today firmly believe in that timeline in spite of the fact that archeologists have proved that Ur, Abraham's place of origin, existed 8000 years ago. Ugarit also was a busy community of more than 7000 people as long ago as 6000 BC. Archeologists also discovered that a great flood had destroyed Ur at about 5000 BC.

As noted above, the writings are not in chronological sequence. And those who study the Scriptures and other cultures know that there was no devil mentioned in the writings until the leaders of Israel were exiled to Babylon in 589-587 BC. While they were there, Persia conquered Babylon and under Persian influence, the Jewish exiles became acquainted with and adopted the Persian god of evil, the great Satan. The

Exiles brought the concept back home when Cyrus granted them their freedom. Before then, God had an assistant who tested people's faith, an advocate, as we see in the beginning of Job. The story of Job was added to when the exiles returned from Babylon. The Greek concept of dualism (a good spirit and a bad spirit), dark opposed to light, flesh opposed to spirit, helped cement this idea of a Devil when the Greeks conquered Israel around 333 BC.

The Persian symbol of Satan was the snake, whom we see appear in the Garden of Eden at the Judgment Tree. A talking snake, in fact, that tempted Eve. This Greek, Roman, and Persian pagan concept of dualism thus found its way into Judaism and developed even further in the intertestamental period in the Apocryphal writings and became full blown by the time of Jesus. Jesus tried to get rid of the idea by saying that he "saw Satan fall like lightning from heaven" (Luke 10:18), but the concept was too anchored in the culture and people would rather have a scapegoat than accept full responsibility for bad decisions. Still, Hell was a long time coming. It never got into the Bible until after the 1500s AD. The notion of Hell came from the Germanic and Norse pagan religions. Luther was the first one to use the concept in his German translation of the Scriptures. But that is another story.

There was no Old Testament, even in the time of Jesus. They did have the Greek translation of writings called the Septuagint. Nevertheless, the writings were not recognized as canonized or official writings.

When we speak of the official, or the valid canon of Scriptures, what do we mean? Canon comes from the Greek word *kanon*, which literally means "reed." It meant a straight rod that was used for measuring something or meeting a standard. When applied to writings, it meant that certain criteria needed to be met for the writing to be acceptable. In other words, they did not begin by assuming that the writings were specially given, but rather, whether they contained truths worthy of acceptance.[23] In the first centuries BC and AD, the religious leaders venerated the writings as Scripture because they were "handed down" by the fathers, e.g., Ben Sirach's grandson, who also believed his grandfather's writings should be included.[24]

The Septuagint, the Greek or Hellenistic texts gathered and translated into Greek for the Alexandrian Jews, contains all the writings that are in the Hebrew Bible. However, the writings are in a different order and it also contains writings that are not in the Hebrew Bible, including Ecclesiastes (or Ben Sirach), Judith, I Maccabees, I Esdras, Tobit, Wisdom of Solomon, Baruch, II Maccabees, Susanna, The Song of the Three Children, Bel and the Dragon, Prayer of Manassas, and III and IV Maccabees. This shows that, since many of these writings were not included in later collections, there was no fixed canon at that time and furthermore, later contemplation excluded some that had been accepted.[25] The Samaritans also have a Pentateuch, which is similar to the Septuagint Pentateuch, but none of the three—the Septuagint, the Samaritan, and the Jewish Pentateuch—is exactly the same in the choice of which writings were acceptable.[26]

The Bible has authority because of the self-evident truths and practical applications gradually clarified by continued relationships with God. God's gradual self-disclosure is culminated in the Scriptures by the coming of Christ. This kind of revelation is what the Synod of Rabbis at Jamnia (as well as the third Council of Carthage) looked for in evaluating which writings had authority in 397.[27] Some Rabbis had started a school at Jamnia after the Temple was destroyed in AD 70. At a Synod in AD 90, they discussed various popular writings and several were heavily debated. Many did not want to include Ezekiel because it had too many discrepancies with the law. They did not want to include Song of Solomon because of its vulgarity. They did not want to include Ecclesiastes because it was shocking with its skepticism and irreverence, and Esther never mentioned God. However, these writings finally squeaked through. Nevertheless, many of the writings, even though eluded to in the Scriptures themselves, were rejected, such as the Book of Jashar, the Book of the Wars of Yahweh, the Book of the Acts of Solomon, the Chronicles of the Kings of Judah, the Chronicles of the Kings of Israel, and the Proclamation of Josiah. Still, even at this time, this Synod did not set the canon.

The choosing of the writings in the Old Testament was a process that went on for centuries after the birth of Christ. Had there been any idea at all that God had given them, there would have been no debate. The discussions were always about the revelations that were revealed in the writings themselves. Incidentally, this Synod added seven books that were not in the Septuagint. The Septuagint was a Greek translation of a collection of old writings that was accomplished by a group of more than 70 scholars starting around 250 BC. It was not completed until about 75 BC. Our present Old Testament does not include these seven books.

Also worth considering is that the Gemara is the part of the Talmud that comprises the rabbinical analysis and commentary on the Mishnah. Although the Mishnah was assembled between AD 180 and 200, and the three separations of the writings were agreed upon and recorded, it still was not settled as to whether certain writings were to be included or rejected. In fact, according to the Gemara, discussions and decisions about certain writings were still being debated in the fourth century AD.[28] Yadayim 3:5 of the Mishnah reveals that there was still a dispute over the inclusion of Ecclesiastes and Song of Songs. The Gemara shows that some still did not admit Proverbs, Esther, Ezekiel, and Ruth although the Mishnah included them all. Even though, as we saw above, Baruch was not included in the collection of Scriptures, in Origen's time (184-253), Baruch was included in the Hebrew writings as Scripture.[29] (Origen was a bishop and church father before Augustine, and was later made a saint.)

Regarding the belief that the Scriptures were translated from the original texts, our Old Testament Scriptures, in fact, were put together with parts of copies of copies of several texts from several different manuscripts—Alexandrian, Aramaic, Masoretic, Syriac, Hebrew, Coptic, the Targum, etc. Our Old Testament did not come from one original source. The preface to the Bible or the footnotes in the Bible explains that this is true.

Another problem lies with the concept of a literal translation. Those who know anything about translating know that it is often impossible to translate literally from one language to another, especially from a graphic type of language like Hebrew. There is simply no such thing as a literal translation of Scripture. We also have the problem that the Bible is a library, or collection of many types of writings; that is what *biblyos* means. This library includes stories, as already mentioned, parables, biographies, songs, poems, prose, allegories, metaphors, lists, laws, history, legends, sermons, etc. Different types of literature have different purposes and therefore different kinds of authority, application, and interpretation.

Too often it is assumed that all who call themselves Christians approach Scripture the same way; we do not, as I have discussed. Some believe that since both the Old Covenant and the New Covenant were given by God, they therefore have equal standing. Others believe that since the old way did not work and Jesus had to come to set us on the right path, that the New Covenant supersedes the old way; therefore, the New Testament informs a better understanding of the Old Testament.

We can see again and again, through the flood story, the proclamations of the prophets (like Isaiah, Amos, Micah, and Hosea), and the exile in 589 BC, that God was very upset with the way his people were living their lives. They all tell us that the old way did not work! Isaiah proclaimed that a new leader would come with a new way. So it was, Jesus was born and named Emmanuel, "God is with us." And we note, in fact, that Jesus was very upset with the religious leaders who were not able to apply the law justly.[30]

Nor can humans save themselves by successfully following the law. That issue had been a problem from the very beginning. The story of Adam and Eve in the Garden teaches that we should not eat from the judgment tree. The story goes on to reveal why. The very first thing the couple did after eating the fruit of the tree was to be ashamed of each other's nakedness, their sexuality. As a result, they judged each other negatively. However, the Genesis 2:5 story tells us, "They were naked and not ashamed." Thus began the ages-long debate and cover-up starting with fig leaves in Gen. 3 and growing into man-made dogmas concerning the transmission of sin, the proper use of semen, etc. The Scriptures themselves teach us that laws, doctrines, and dogma are not successful in changing people for the better. It takes much more than regulations to make a real difference in people's lives. I will delve further into this later in the book.

To complicate things even more, we too often misapply texts to serve our own purposes. Peter Geiger illustrates this in the following story, "Some Bible Preaching."

> There was a fellow filled with such great zeal that he felt that he had been called upon to preach. He applied for examination to the appropriate council in his denomination. The examination proceeded as follows:
>
> "Can you read, Sam?"
>
> "No, sir."
>
> "Can you write?"
>
> "No, sir, but my wife can."
>
> "Well, what will you preach if you make a minister, Sam?"
>
> "I won't preach nothin' that ain't in the Bible. In fact, I'm pretty good in the Bible. I know the Bible from lid to lid."
>
> "What part of the Bible do you like best?"
>
> "The New Testament."
>
> "What book?"
>
> "The Book of Parables, sir."

"What parable?"

"The parable of the Good Samaritan."

"Well, go ahead, Sam, give us a short message on the Good Samaritan."

"Well, sir, a man was going down from Jerusalem to Jericho and he fell among thieves. And thorns grew up and choked that man. He didn't have no script for his purse. And behold, he met the Queen of Sheba and behold, she gave that man—yes, sir—she gave that man a thousand talents of gold and a hundred changes of raiment and said, 'Take no thought for what you shall put on.' And he got in a chariot straight away and drove furiously. And as he was speedin' along, his hair got caught in a limb and left him hangin' there asleep. His wife, Delilah, came along and cut off his hair and the poor man dropped down and fell on stony ground. Then it began to rain and it rained for forty days and forty nights and he hid himself in a cave until the rain stopped. And when he came out of the cave he met a man who said, 'Come in and take supper with me.' But he said, 'No, I done married me a wife and I can't come.' So the man went out on the highways and byways and compelled them to come for supper. So the first man went and came to Jericho. And when he got there, he saw Queen Jezebel sittin' high up in the window. And when he saw her he said, 'Throw her down.' And they threw her down some more. And they threw her down seventy times seven until she went all to pieces on the ground. And from the fragments, they picked up twelve baskets full. Now, in the resurrection, who all's wife is she gonna be?"

Many people are extremely careless about how they read and use texts from Scripture. They take them out of the context in which they were written and use them for authority to back up anything under the sun.

Furthermore, translators confuse us because they use the word "sin" as a translation of two distinct concepts without differentiating between them: *anomia*, which has to do with sins of violation of law and justice, and *bdeleguma*, which has to do with infringement of ritual purity or monotheistic worship. Both are sins but they carry different consequences. Translators also change words to fit the changing culture, not always keeping faith with the original meaning; for example, changing young maid to virgin, or male prostitute to homosexual, or change of mind or direction to repentance. At the same time, we must acknowledge that some words do change meanings through cultural usage and time (inn for guest room, suffer vs. allow, sodomy and sodomite, servant or slave, etc.).

One word that ties in with sexuality issues is the word *pornia*. Translators, commentators, and those with particular biases have had a field day with it. It has been used to mean everything from sexual indiscretions to pornography, from fornication to adultery to homosexuality, and more. This word has been misused all through church history and certainly today. However, its original meaning had to do with the worship rituals for fertility gods and goddesses. It is important to keep the original meaning in mind rather than just use the word willy-nilly.

Also, as referred to above, four different schools of writers wrote Bible texts from their perspectives. The Yahwists, from the Southern Kingdom, used the name Yahweh for God and wrote from the time of Solomon to Eliljah, about 950 to 850 BC. The Elohists, whose history goes back before Abraham, were from the Northern Kingdom. They, of course, used the name Elohim, plural for the fertility cult El gods, and wrote from about 750 BC to the time of Amos and Hosea. The Deuteronomists wrote the Law Code during the 600s BC and included essentially Deuteronomy, Judges, and Kings. Last, the Priestly writers wrote during and after the exile, from about 550-450 BC. They wrote parts of Exodus, Numbers, Leviticus, and Job, as well as the Genesis 1 Sabbath story, often referred to as one of the Creation stories.[31] Their purpose in Gen. 1f. was to emphasize the importance of keeping the Sabbath. How do we know who wrote when? Fortunately, one huge help is the fact that Hebrew and Greek alphabetical letters changed shapes through the centuries, helping us to identify the period in which the various portions were written. The subject matter also helps, as does the types of words used.

The Pentateuch, later misnamed "The Books of Moses," which includes much of Genesis through Deuteronomy, did not begin to be written until some 300 years after Moses lived.

During the 400s BC, various writings and stories were redacted, or brought together. The writers did not always agree on what happened where or when. I have already mentioned the Ten Commandments, and many stories use both Yahweh and Elohim, revealing that someone brought stories from different times together into one and included perspectives from different times and cultures.

How we bring together our ideas about God and how God interacts in history forms our theology. So how does all of this affect your theology?

Where does our religious history begin? It begins with Abram, later named Abraham after his blessing. Abram, or Abraham, is considered our first Patriarch. Depending on the scholar you read, Abram lived anywhere from 2200 to 1800 BC. Abram's family lived first in Ur, near Babylon, at the mouth of the Euphrates River, and then moved 600 miles to Haran at the other end of the Euphrates, then, finally, several hundred miles down to Canaan. Both Ur and Haran were centers of worship for the moon god, Sin or Nana, depending on location.

Abram called God "the Shield of Abraham" (Genesis15:11) and worshipped at the "high places," as did all the Patriarchs. The high places were centers of worship for the Baal fertility cult gods. The Scriptures make it clear that Abram's gods were Elohim when he dwelt in Canaan. He went up to a high place to sacrifice his son, Isaac, to Elohim (Genesis 22:1-12).

Furthermore, we are told that the first altar built after the flood was constructed at a high place (Genesis 8:20). Laban and Jacob built an altar on Mt. Gilead (Genesis 31:54). Jacob's wife, Rachel, stole her father's household gods (*teraphim*; Genesis 31:19, 34, 35), which were used in the worship of Asherah or Athirat. Some believe the teraphim were phallic symbols. Even King David had teraphim in his home (1 Samuel 19:13-

16). Rachel named her first son Aher, after the goddess who was the consort of the moon god. In ancient Ugarit, Asherah was the consort of El and Baal was one of her sons. In Judges, we can see that the Israelites made use of teraphim even in the Temple (2 Kings 23:6) and in Hosea, the text declares a time when they will not be used. Later, teraphim are prohibited. Asherah and the teraphim were worshipped until the sixth century BC. So, the god to which one is referring depends on where in the Old Testament one finds the reference.

When the Israelites learned about Yahweh and came back to the promised land from Egypt, they were ordered to destroy all the high places (Exodus 34:13; Deut. 7:5; Deut. 12:2, etc.). They were forbidden to worship at these centers (Deut. 12:11-14). However, it wasn't just the Patriarchs who worshipped these fertility gods; they were worshipped in both Israel and Judah down until Samuel and Ahab at places like Shechem, Shiloh, Bethel, and, yes, Bethlehem. That is long after Yahweh was made known and the law was given. In fact, this worship of Elohist gods went on for some 2000 years. These pagan worship rituals were still going on in the time of Paul, as we shall see.

For most Jews, there came a time when there was only one place to go to worship, where sacrifices were made, at the Temple (Leviticus 17:34; Deut. 12; 16:21). Yet 2 Kings14:4; 15:4; 35:21; 2 Chronicles 16:17; and others tell us that fertility cult worship was still occurring. The Samaritans worshipped at the Temple on Mt. Gerizim until it was destroyed in 128 BC.

Why do the Scriptures name so many gods if the one and only God gave us the Scriptures? Each name has a specific meaning and specific attributes, such as:

Abraham = Shield of Abraham, Genesis 15:11

Isaac = Fear of Isaac, Genesis 31:42, 53

Jacob = Strong one of Jacob, Genesis 49:2

Still, they honored and used the names of the Elohim or Baal deities, such as:

Adonai = Deity of vegetation, especially corn, Isaiah 17:10

El = Power (after Jacob wrestled at the Jabbok, he named the place Peniel, or "the Face of El"), Genesis 32:30

El Shaddai = All powerful or almighty, destructive violence, Genesis 17:1, 28:3, Numbers 24:4 etc. In Job it is used 31 times.

Elohim = Plural gods expressed in many ways in nature: springtime, winter, sun, moon, storms, growth, etc., Judges 9:13; Exodus 12:12; Exodus 18:11; Exodus 20:3; Deut. 10:17; 1 Samuel 4:8; 2 Samuel 7:23; Psalms 86:8[32]

El Elyon = Power most high, Genesis 14:18-20

El Olam = Power eternal, Genesis 21:23

El Roi = Power who sees, Genesis 16:13-14

Bethel = Place or home of El

Bethlehem = house or place of the god Lahemu (god of grain)

To urge these gods to function as needed, the people participated in sexual rituals. One of the practices of some of these fertility cult religions was to sacrifice one's firstborn son. So, we have Abraham taking his son,

Isaac, up to a high place to sacrifice him to Elohim (Genesis 22:1-19). However, Abraham had a revelation that a ram could be substituted for his son, and this began a new trend in Judaism of sacrificing sheep, doves, goats, bulls, and grain, rather than humans, until the destruction of the Temple in AD 70.

Ironically, even the country Israel got its name from the Elohim gods. Recall that Jacob was filled with guilt as he went to meet up with his brother, Esau. Jacob had stolen Esau's birthright and was afraid that Esau was coming to take his revenge on Jacob. He discovered that his brother was coming with a large number of people, so Jacob sent his family on ahead while he stayed the night by the Jabbok River. As Jacob anxiously waited for the meeting, tortured by his guilt, he found himself wrestling with the god El during the night. Having survived the struggle, Jacob named the place Peniel, meaning the place where he saw El. Because of this experience, Jacob's name was changed to Israel, meaning "he wrestled El." Jacob became Israel. Israel became a tribe. The tribe became the Northern Kingdom. Thus, the country of Yahweh's chosen people is named "He wrestled El," after pagan fertility gods.

Again, what we see happening with Jacob's name is called an eponym. Adam and Eve have already been noted as representing mankind and womankind. Jacob became all Israel; his sons became the 12 tribes of Israel; his brother Esau became Edom. Genesis 25:23 states, "There are two nations in your womb," referring to Rebecca. The cities of Hamor and Shechem were the father and son Amalek and Moab; Leah and Rachel represented two nations; and Laban was Syria. Judah got its name from the place where the Baal god Jeduh was worshipped,[33] which became the Southern Kingdom (Genesis 25:23). Those who were of this tribe were called Jude, later Jew, and eventually, we have the Jewish faith, Judaism. Many times when we are reading the Patriarchs' names, we do not realize that we have switched from a person to an entire tribe, or even a nation.

How one perceives God to be guides how the person behaves. Moses believed people could live as God wanted by following rules. Joshua believed in a God who wanted all those who did not believe like him to be destroyed. Under Joshua we had the first recorded holocaust, a war that lasted some hundred years. While Scripture reveals that God creates us in his likeness, it is how one views that likeness that determines one's beliefs and behavior. What attributes do you give to God? You have a vast array from which to choose in Scripture. And what you choose will be who you are. Some say, "Who you are selects the kind of god you choose." We claim that we believe in one God. Nevertheless, because of the different attributes different people give to God, it is as though they follow different gods.

The Scriptures reveal the change from some thousand years of fertility cult polytheism to monotheism under Yahweh. Circumcision was chosen as a rite of covenant with Yahweh and a symbol of community unity, and this is interesting because both traditions that introduced circumcision are from the fertility cults.

The first introduction to this rite was when Ishmael was born. Because Elohim granted Abraham a son at the age of about 100 years, Abraham made a special covenant with Elohim by circumcising both Ishmael and himself (Genesis 17:24-27). The other instance is by way of

Zipporah, Moses' wife who was the daughter of the Midianite priest. Midian was the fourth son of Abraham by his wife Keturah. Numbers 25:3 informs us that the Midianites worshipped Baal-peor and Numbers 31:16 states that they performed obscene rites. Zipporah married Moses while he was seeking safe haven with her family after murdering the Egyptian taskmaster. As Moses was sleeping one night, while taking his family with him back to Egypt, Zipporah believed this new God, Yahweh, who was foreign to her, was going to kill Moses during the night. She circumcised their son and touched Moses "feet" with the foreskin to protect him (Exodus 4:24-26).

Joshua extended the use of circumcision when he had all the men make a special covenant and be circumcised before they crossed the Jordan back into the promised land (Joshua 5:2-9). Circumcision was established as a national ordinance representing their joint commitment to their faith (Genesis 17:10,11). The rite of circumcision is another connection of the sexual with the holy. However, the Christians cancelled the rite as we see in Galatians 6:15 and Colossians 3:11. If they had believed that the rite was given by God, they would not have dared to have cancelled it.

This intermingling with the fertility cults continued right up through the time of Paul after the death and resurrection of Jesus. The texts we have in Romans, Corinthians, and Timothy concerning these rites have been dishonestly misappropriated and used to condemn same-sex relationships.

What do we mean when we say the Bible is God's Word? A big part of our problem has to do with what we mean by "holy" or "sacred." It is evident that the first thousand years of biblical heritage was constructed on belief in the supernatural. The many gods had to do with people trying to cope with different aspects of nature: seeding time, growth, harvest, seasons, storms, etc. That type of religion slowly advanced to the concept of the holy other, one God over all. Holy and sacred are terms that we have applied to our reverence, loyalty, and respect for our God. It has to do with our honoring God. The Bible writings were created and selected to remind us of our heritage of the struggle to know God's way and to guide us in our relationship with God. Because they relate us to the Holy One, they are sacred. They are not writings that God handed down to us.

From the very beginning of our religious journey, fertility/sexuality has been a most important connection with God. If one thinks about the purpose of the fertility cults, the importance of fertility is not too surprising. If your crops and livestock did not do well, you might very well starve to death. If you did not have enough children, you not only did not have enough affordable labor to work your crops and flocks, you also had no security in your old age, should you live so long. Fertility was a huge, very important issue!

In fact, the sex organs were considered a direct link to God's way of continuing life in more than one way. Not only was it essential that the family, the tribe, the community, the crops, and the herds increase, it was through one's descendants that one continued on after death. People did not know about the resurrection that we know today.

As God was holy, so were the sex organs. Because the sex organs were used as God's way to continue the human race—and all living things—they, too, were holy, sacred. Just as God's name was so holy that it could not be pronounced, the penis, testicles, and vagina could not be named, either. Euphemisms like "feet" and "thigh" were used instead. Today, one is not to mention them because they are viewed negatively, as "dirty." We have gone from holy to embarrassing and now to dirty in our thinking. We began a downhill slide with Origen's and Augustine's false view of the incident at the judgment tree in the garden of Eden.

Zipporah touched Moses' "feet" (Genesis 49:10; Exodus 4:25; Ruth 3:4). Ruth uncovered Boaz's "feet" and became pregnant. If one is a witness in court today, one puts one's hand on the Bible, or testament. In the time of the Patriarchs, to make a vow or covenant with another person, one would place his hand on the other's testicles (Genesis 24:2; 24:9; 32;25; 47:29). Thus we get "testament." Sex connected one to the sacred, but now, too often, sex has bad connotations. What a difference! The Old Covenant people had a much healthier attitude about sex than do many in our culture. Don't forget, the end of the original creation story in Genesis 2:25 states that God created men and women and that "they were naked and they were not ashamed." And we are told in the other creation story, "God saw that all was good."

As for marriage, the Bible includes polygamous, concubinal, monogamous, Levarite, matriarchal, and patriarchal marriages, and exogamy (marriage outside your social group) and endogamy (marriage within your social or religious group). Several of these are illegal today.

Not only do cultures change, but many people today select and manipulate Scripture to their purpose just as the Scribes and Pharisees did. Jesus objected to that approach. Also, many people neglect that which does not fit their purpose. Too many read the Scriptures selectively. They pick out texts that suit their biases and neglect the rest. To what they select, they give special authority; what they neglect is of no importance to them.

Even in the Bible, ethics are not always clear. Take Abraham's dealings with his wife Sarah, for example. Twice he gave her away, first to a pharaoh and then to a king, saying that she was his sister. They found that she was his wife after spending the night with her. They were the ones feeling embarrassed and they paid off Abraham to make things right (Genesis 12:18 and Genesis 20). Ironically, she actually was his sister!

Moses united the tribes under one God, Yahweh, and tried to build a righteous society by a system of laws with assistance from his father-in-law, who was a Baal priest. As we have seen, this way failed. Laws from without are not enough. As Jeremiah proclaimed, "Circumcision of the foreskin is not enough. One must have a circumcised heart" (Jeremiah 9:23-26). When Stephen was arrested and taken before the Council, he confronted the legalists with the same issue. He said, "You stiff necked people, uncircumcised in heart—you are forever opposing the Holy Spirit. You received the law but did not keep it" (Acts 7:51f). They stoned him to death. The people also used the law to torture to death one as perfect as Jesus. Furthermore, Paul, who was well trained in the law before his conversion, confirmed that "real circumcision (commitment) is a matter of the heart—it is spiritual and not literal" (Romans 2:28-29).

History, tradition, experience, and Jesus showed that the people could neither live righteous lives nor save themselves through laws. Since that system failed, God sent Jesus with the good news of love, forgiveness, reconciliation, and grace—an entirely different approach to living.

The Scriptures show our slow development in understanding our relationship to God and one another. So, you say, "No matter what they called Him, there is only one God," and I agree. Nevertheless, those different names carried very different attributes, different understandings, at different times. Those understandings went from some 1500 gods, to one among many, to, finally, one God. Those understandings went all the way from many gods desiring sexually obscene rituals, behavior leading to war, a destructive god, and human sacrifice, to a God of complete love. How we understand, accept, and apply the attributes of God make a world of difference.

So, from all this, what does one mean by "the Word of God?" It is apparent that literalism and legalism are judgmental and destructive and did not work. The very first story, after the creation stories, warns us to stay away from the fruit of the judgment tree. With this background of approaching the Word of God, and with the warning of Jesus in mind concerning the Pharisees', Sadducees', and Scribes' misuse of Scripture (that is, to take Scriptures out of context to use for another purpose), our next chapter examines texts that have been used against homosexuals.

Chapter 5

Misusing Scriptural Texts

Scriptural Texts Used Against Homosexuals

With the last chapter in mind, let us look at some texts that have been claimed to inform us about homosexuality. Before we start, we should face the fact that the concept of homosexuality did not exist before 1869, when K. M. Benkert invented the concept in Germany.[34] The word did not appear in any Bible until 1952, in the RSV of all places! Since 1989, that translation has gone back to the correct translation of Scripture.

Furthermore, the definition of homosexuality has changed several times since1869. It has gone all the way from being defined as a "sick practice," to a "preference" for the same sex, to an "emotional and physical" need for the same sex.

For those who do not accept the decision of the first Church Council in Acts 15, that the Old Covenant laws no longer apply (with four exceptions), let's look at some favorite Old Testament texts that are used to denigrate, even attack homosexuals.

Genesis 19 presents the Sodom and Gomorrah Story (see references also in Ezekiel 16:49 and Luke 10:10). In this story, God had already decided to destroy the community before the two angels came to town—yes, before that particular incident. The previous chapter sets the stage as Abraham was singled out for showing these angels hospitality (Genesis 18:18f.). Hospitality is the whole point of the story, as is pointed out in several books of the Old Testament and by Jesus in Luke 10:10f.

Anyone who is at all aware of the customs of the day knows that, first of all, strangers were to be referred to the elders at the gate to be interviewed so the elders could decide how best to help the sojourner; and second, that Lot was an alien in their community who interfered with this custom.

Remember, there were no Motel 8s or Holiday Inns.

Furthermore, according to a rabbinical exegesis known as Tosefta Sota, the affluent people of Sodom selfishly adopted a policy of maltreating strangers in order to discourage visitors from staying in their city (Tosefta Sota 3:11-12). Inhospitality was the problem and this is confirmed again and again by the Wisdom of Solomon 19:14-15; Matthew 10:12-15; and in Josephus's *Antiquities* 1 ¶194. It had nothing to do with the modern definition of homosexuality.

Indeed, when the people of Sodom come to Lot's house, the word they use in connection with wanting to see the strangers is *yadha*, "to get to know." Yadha is used 943 times in the Old Testament. Out of all those times, it is used only 10 times in a sexual connotation, and all of those refer to heterosexual relationships. Furthermore, the people who came to Lot's house were men, women, and children. This was not the type of setting for having any kind of sex. Perhaps it was Lot, the alien, who misunderstood their intent, and then offered his daughters to them. In any case, the final act was an act of heterosexual mob violence against Lot's daughters. It had absolutely nothing to do with same-sex relationships. Note, again, what is stated in the Scriptures: in Ezekiel 16:49-50 and Wisdom 19:13-14, the sin is inhospitality. Jesus, in Luke 10, said, "But whenever you enter a town and they do not receive you, go into its streets and say, 'Even the dust of your town that clings to our feet, we wipe off against you, it shall be more tolerable on that day for Sodom than for that town.'"

Jude did see a sexual issue, but it was not homosexuality, as he makes clear. The sin is seen as fornication with angels. As the Jerusalem Bible footnotes it, "They lusted not after human beings, but after the strangers who were angels." The Scriptures are not in agreement as to the problem. However, to state that this has anything at all to do with homosexuality directly contradicts what the Bible itself declares.

When "sodomy" is referred to in Isaiah 1:10 and 3:9, the problem is injustice. In Jeremiah 23:14, Sodom and Gomorrah are associated with general wickedness, e.g., adultery, lies, and injustice. In Ezekiel 16:49, Sodom represents pride, excess of food, prosperous ease, and indifference to the poor and needy. Nowhere is homosexuality or same-sex relationships named as the particular wickedness that warrants destruction. In fact, nowhere in the Bible is the sin of Sodom referred to as same-sex acts.

Evangelical Bible scholar William H. Brownlee (1917-1983) was a leading American Bible scholar. He was a junior Fellow at the American Schools of Oriental Research in Jerusalem when the Dead Sea Scrolls were discovered. As the scrolls were brought to the school when its director was away, it was Brownlee and John Trever, the other junior Fellow, who first realized the scrolls' age and importance. Brownlee published many works on the Dead Sea Scrolls. He became professor of Religion at Claremont Graduate School and director of their Dead Sea Scrolls Project, retiring in 1982. In the Word Biblical Commentary on Ezekiel 1-19, Brownlee explains that the word sodomy in Genesis meant basically "oppression of the weak and helpless; and the oppression of the stranger."

Joshua 6 is another text misused by homophobic people. It is a parallel story to Genesis 19 and an eloquent testimony to the paramount importance of hospitality. The city of Jericho, like Sodom, was completely destroyed by the Lord, and the one person spared was a prostitute, although prostitution is prohibited in both Leviticus (19:29) and Deuteronomy (23:17). Why was she saved? It was because she offered hospitality to the messengers of Joshua. Hospitality, again, is the issue.

Another well known linguist, Yale's John Boswell, notes, "Sodom is used as a symbol of evil in dozens of places in the Bible—but not in a single instance is the sin of the Sodomites specified as same-sex relations, or today's concept of homosexuality. If, as the many references in the Scriptures themselves point out, it was punishment for inhospitality, isn't it ironic that perhaps the group with whom the Christian Church, in recent years, has been most inhospitable is the homosexual?"

Why is heterosexual violence used to argue against homosexual love? This is especially troubling when we look at texts such as the story of the rape of Dinah by the Shechemites (Genesis 34), or the rape of Tamar by Amnon (2 Samuel 13), or when we read the story of David's adultery with Bathsheba (2 Samuel 2). In these texts, we identify the issue as injustice or the abuse of power, as the parable of Nathan makes clear in 2 Samuel 12:1-15. These are all heterosexual acts—and terrible ones—but we certainly do not question the legitimacy of heterosexuality. We do not say that heterosexuality is wrong because of these acts. What makes the difference?

Some people like to use the later story of creation (Genesis 1:1f) as a basis for arguing against homosexuality. They point out that sex is for procreation and homosexuality does not provide for procreation. However, the creation story in Genesis 1 does not speak of husband and wife or even man and woman. It speaks of male and female in a biological sense, mankind and womankind. We are made in the image of God and compared to other creatures God has made. It does not speak about orientation here. Those who like to play with words and say "God made Adam and Eve, not Adam and Steve," are not even aware of—or choose to ignore—the meanings of the words Adam and Eve, let alone what this Scripture really means.

Let us remember that "Adam and Eve" are eponyms, as are many names in Scripture, and that is a whole study in itself. Adam and Eve are words for the creation of mankind and womankind. All through the Old

Testament, groups of people are personified with individual names to get the story across. How do you think Cain, after killing Abel, was able to go down into the next valley and marry if they were the only people on earth?

This Genesis text celebrates God's deliberate and equal creation of persons who are male and persons who are female. Such a sense of equal creation was not typical in the ancient world, according to Professor Douglas J. Miller of Eastern Baptist Seminary. He wrote, "Crude natural law ideas are…read into…the early chapters of Genesis. … This view [supports] the 'physicalist' ethical model upon which heterosexism is built. … This view of creation is based upon the obvious anachronism of reading 13th-century definitions of nature into ancient Hebrew texts." Those who use Genesis 1:27 against homosexuals should note Paul's statement in Galatians 3:28, in which he is emphatic that there is now no theological significance to the heterosexual pair "male and female." According to evangelical Pauline scholar F. F. Bruce, "Paul states the basic principle here; if restrictions on the meaning of male and female are found elsewhere…they are to be understood in relation to Galatians 3:28, and not vice versa."

Why would one emphasize the procreation story over the companionship story of creation? Procreation is not a command that every human being can keep. Some people are biologically incapable of bearing children. There are those who, for economical and other reasons, cannot see their way clear to have children. "Be fruitful and multiply" comes not only out of a need to continue the human race, but also out of cultural conditions of the day for caring for one's property, building up equity, and ensuring security for the parents in their older years. Using procreation as the main issue neglects the older creation story that speaks of the importance of companionship. In the original story in Genesis 2, human beings are related to in sociological terms and there it is clear that we are created for companionship. Procreation is not even a part of the original story. If what came first gives the most authority, then companionship should be more important than procreation. Jesus himself broke the procreation command: we know of no children by him. Procreation is a big deal in this story because it is a fertility cult story. If procreation is so critically important, why are the clergy of the largest branch of the Christian church required to make a high spiritual commitment to be celibate? Does that old law still hold? Should all these religious leaders be put to death for not holding to the dogma of procreation?

Nor is the Deuteronomy text (23:17-18) about homosexuality. It is about cult prostitution as we can plainly see in the use of the words *kedesha* and *kadesh*, which mean literally "holy" and "sacred." The King James version included Sodom here, but it was not originally a part of this text. The references here are to Canaanite priest-prostitutes practicing their fertility cult rituals. Again, this has absolutely nothing to do with same-sex relationships.

Other texts that have been used to decry homosexuality include 1 Kings 14:24 and 15:12, and 2 Kings 23:7. However, these texts refer to prostitution, false worship, and idolatry. Within the Hebrew texts, the term has changed from *qades* to *teletes*, meaning "initiating priest," priests who are ceremonially unclean. These Scriptures say absolutely nothing about homosexuality or same-sex relationships.

But the most popular Old Testament texts used against homosexuals today are Leviticus 18:22 and 20:13f. The first thing to know about the text in Leviticus 18 is that it is not a complete sentence and, as a result, no honest translator knows what it means. The closest literal translation used by Christians is, "thou shalt not lie the lyings of a woman..."

The second thing one needs to realize is that this section has to do with the holiness code in connection with priests forbidden to participate in idol worship as participated in by the Canaanites and the Egyptians. The phrase *to evah ha goyim* is repeated again and again. This phrase has to do specifically with idol worship.

In both the Talmud and Maimonides' commentary on Leviticus 18:23, the phrase "You shall not sleep the sleep of a woman with a man" (the literal translation in the Jewish tradition), refers specifically to the Kadeshim and they are labeled as "to evah"—definitely aimed at condemning temple prostitution as we see in Kings 14:24.[35]

The part having to do with men "lying the lyings of women," may mean the mixing of sex roles, which was thought to be polluting. But both Jesus and Paul reject all such ritual distinctions, as we see in Mark 7:17-23, "It is what comes from within the heart that defiles a person" and Romans 14:14, 20, "Nothing is unclean in itself." Lest you think this is just liberal rationalization, even the *Fundamentalist Journal* declares that this holiness code (chapters 17-26) condemns "idolatrous practices" and "ceremonial uncleanness." and states, "'Abomination' (to evah) is a technical cultic term for what is ritually unclean, such as mixed cloth, pork, and intercourse with menstruating women." It's not about a moral or ethical issue. According to the *Fundamentalist Journal*, which is no flaming liberal document, "We are not bound by these commands today" (see Evangelicals Concerned, Inc., http://ecinc.org/).

The third thing that one should face up to is the list of other practices under the same law that were named as abominations, such as: eating meat with blood in it, 18:19; having sex with a menstruating woman, 19:19b; planting more than one type of seed in the same field, 20:12; wearing clothes made of anything other than one pure natural fiber, eating pork, and cutting one's hair. Also, one was to kill children who slighted their parents. A person crippled in any way could not enter the worship area.

These laws have a definite cultural concern about cultic purity and proper worship as then defined. That is why the Hebrew word "to evah" and the phrase "to evah ha goyim" are interspersed throughout—which means, as already stated, that all these laws have to do with idol worship. These laws are not about moral or ethical issues. Again, these laws in Leviticus18:23 and 20:13 (both from the holiness code for priests, contrasting pagan worship of fertility gods) have their purpose specified in Leviticus 20:23, "And you shall not walk in the customs of the nation which I am casting out before you; for they did all these things, and therefore I abhorred them."

If, in spite of the facts, one chooses to follow this ancient law, then one should be consistent. Do you eat meat cooked medium or rare? Do you eat pork? If so, this law says you should be put to death. Do you plant several vegetables in the same garden? You should be put to death.

Do you wear clothes made of synthetic fiber, even mixed synthetic fibers? If you do any of these, you either do not really believe in this law, or you couldn't care less. The point is, why force a law on someone else if it has no meaning for you, even if the original writers did mean homosexuality? And especially, why follow laws rejected in Acts 15?

Robert L. Brawley writes, "While most people do not accept most of these prohibitions, there are those who hold onto the one about the 'lyings of a woman.' Why would anyone say that one certain part of these laws applies today but just about all the rest do not? On what basis are those decisions made? Why is one prohibition insisted upon while all the others are out-and-out rejected? Why is it that, when some nations today practice the *lex talionis*, or the law of retaliation ("an eye for an eye, a tooth for a tooth"), many other nations consider it incompatible with modern morality?"[36]

Marten H. Woudstra, a Calvin Theological Seminary Old Testament scholar, says, "There is nothing in the Old Testament that corresponds to homosexuality as we understand it today."

We ordain people who cut their hair or shave; we ordain people who have physical defects. Also, we have decided that the Old Testament dietary laws do not apply. Many people eat their steak cooked medium or rare. Many people eat pork, shrimp, or bullheads. However, according to this law, one is to be put to death if he or she does any of these things. This is the same law that some use against homosexuals. Obviously, there is something else involved in denigrating homosexuals other than just what some claim "the Bible says."

New Testament

Even in reading Scripture, we must not set aside our ability to think, to reason. Must you agree with Paul that it is "unnatural" for a man to grow long hair or for a woman to cut her hair? No! Nor do we agree with the creation argument used by Paul in 1 Timothy 2:11-14 that, since Adam was created before Eve, women must be subordinate to men. If one takes that line of argument to its logical conclusion, one may say that human beings are subordinate to vegetables and animals because vegetables and animals were created first, according to Genesis 1. In other words, "We cannot disregard the historical and cultural context out of which the Bible comes."[37]

Here is another example. As David, in 1 Samuel 21-22, used the holy bread for his men—bread that was declared by law (Leviticus 24:5-9) to be only used by the priests—so Jesus referred to David's example and reinterpreted it still again in regards to Sabbath law. Recall Jesus' famous declaration that the Sabbath was made for humankind and not humankind for the Sabbath (Matthew 12:1-8). Who can deny that Jesus reinterpreted the law again and again to suit the needs of the day? Luke 6:1-5 (picking grain on the Sabbath) is an important guideline for theological thinking. For David and for Jesus, human needs provided the key for understanding. The law was a sign of God's perpetual covenant, as it declares in Exodus 31:15-17; it was not meant to be made absolute. This is where hermeneutics, where one's theology and Christology come in.

The law stated that certain animals and birds could not be eaten, but Acts 10 tells of Peter having a vision that changed the law. Peter took the vision even further and declared that he learned from that experience that he could not call any person common or unclean. While the law declared Gentiles (that's us, folks!) unclean, the coming of Jesus Christ changed all that. Indeed, Jesus brought a New Covenant, a far better way! This new way to live and relate to God IS different from the old.

Peter was taken to task over not keeping the law and had to answer the complaints with the Jerusalem leaders and the circumcision group. The complainers here are male Christians of Jewish background.[38] The content of their complaint is interesting. From Acts 10, we might have guessed that they would object to Peter preaching to Gentiles or, especially, to baptizing them. But what seems to have really set them off is that he ate with these people.[39]

We recall, of course, that Jesus also got in trouble for eating with the wrong sort of people.[40] What seems petty may actually be insightful. These complainers have correctly discerned the implications of Peter's action. Baptizing outsiders means that they cannot be regarded as outsiders anymore. They become people with whom we share life and hospitality. The story about Peter's mission to the Gentiles continues the account that began in Acts 10:1 and it repeats in greater detail the content of Peter's vision in Acts 10:9-16. It is a remarkable story because it treats rather lightly a dispute that was widespread in the New Testament church: the dispute over conditions to be required of Gentile converts to the faith.

The apostle Paul was quite sure that following the Jewish law was no longer incumbent upon any Christians simply because when Christians tried to follow the law, they were depending upon themselves, whereas salvation depended entirely on faith in God's work in Jesus Christ. Thus Paul's whole letter to the church at Galatia strongly condemns those who insist on the necessity of keeping Judaism's laws. "If anyone is preaching to you a different gospel let him be accursed." he writes.[41]

Saint Paul urged Christians not to be entangled again with the yoke of bondage (Mosaic Law).[42] He went so far as to reject circumcision, for example, saying that if Christians did this that, "Christ shall profit you nothing." It is very clear that Levitical regulations had no hold on Christians. In fact, the church took this concept so seriously that a couple of centuries later, it went so far as to declare that anyone who circumcised a person should be put to death! Christians live by faith, not law. Otherwise, one betrays Jesus.

So then, let us look at what the New Testament teaches us about what we call homosexuality. Our biggest problem here is the translators. Rather than translating as literally as possible, they too often try to make the text fit today's culture or, worse, include their own biases. I say this, not because I think my expertise is superior to theirs (although I have studied both classical and Koine Greek), rather, I say it because of comments by ancient language experts whom I trust. It is upon their scholarship that I base the following.

Romans 1:26-27 shares the Old Testament *tebel* and *to evah ha goyim* terms through the Greek word *paraphusin*. To evah ha goyim is usually connected to idol worship, as I discussed above, while tebel has more to do with the concept of mixing; it literally means "to mix" or "go against nature." The Greek paraphusin is closer to the mixing concept. Paul is speaking of heterosexual Christian men and women doing what is unnatural for them by participating in rituals worshipping an idol associated with animals, birds, and reptiles. We know this if we begin reading at verse 23 rather than 26: "Claiming to be wise, they became fools, and they exchanged the glory of the immortal God for images resembling a mortal human being, or birds or four-footed animals, or reptiles. Therefore God gave them up in the lusts of their hearts to impurity, to the degrading of their bodies, among themselves because they exchanged the truth about God for a lie and worshiped and served the creature rather than the Creator who is blessed forever! Amen."

This is very clear. This same word, paraphusin, is used by both Mathew, in 11:8, and Luke, in 7:5, with a totally different connotation. In both those instances, the word is used to describe John's robe as "soft" raiment. Paraphusin has absolutely nothing to do with homosexuality. Thomas Aquinas' use of paraphusin became the basis for the Roman Catholic Church's dogma of natural law. It had absolutely nothing whatsoever to do with same-sex relatonships. I will discuss this further in the section about tradition.

Referring to Romans 1:26-27, Victor Paul Furnish of Southern Methodist University reminds us, "For Paul, neither homosexual practice nor heterosexual promiscuity nor any other specific vice is identified as such with 'sin.' In his view, the fundamental sin from which all particular evils derive is idolatry, worshiping what is created rather than the Creator, be that a wooden idol, an ideology, or a religious system, or some particular moral code." We know this by Paul's own summary in Romans 3:22b-23, "For there is no distinction, since all have sinned and fallen short of the glory of God." Furnish adds, "homosexual practice as such is not the topic under discussion."

Almost all commentators interpret Romans 1:13-3:20 as Paul's preliminary to showing things destructive to the body. But what if sexual behavior is motivated by love, goodness, faithfulness, and such, and is good for the body? The point Paul is trying to make is that everyone sins and it is only by the grace of God through Christ that any of us are saved. Why pick out one act and forget all the rest—even if this text did refer to homosexuality, which it definitely does not. To do so misses the whole point of these three introductory chapters of Romans by Paul.

Again, the first three chapters with their list of sins are intended to show that no one is worthy.[43] Ironically, the argument clearly is directed at those who acknowledge their allegiance to the Mosaic Torah; and here, Jewish reliance on the saving efficacy of God's law is demolished.[44] These first three chapters are intended to show that there is no distinction among people, since all have sinned and fall short of the glory of God; they are, whether Jews, Greeks, or any other group, recipients of God's gracious and unearned justification. Only by God's grace are any of us saved, lest we boast in our own doing. Even pride is listed among these sins. Those who use this text to condemn a person as a sinner have missed the whole point of Paul's writing. Again, his point is that we are all sinners. We cannot save ourselves. We are saved by God's grace.

Paul's whole point is to firmly establish the basis of faith justification over against legal rectitude. By faith alone is one saved. Pious stereotyping condemns the one who condemns. Christ died for ALL! God so loved the world as is proclaimed in John 3:16. The teachings of

Christ are based on grace, not works. He did, however, put much emphasis on fruit and we know from this perspective that faith without works is dead—but that is all to a very different purpose. We are not saved by good works; rather, if we are saved, it is our works—doing good, results—which show that we are saved.

In Romans 1, Paul is ridiculing pagan religious rebellion, saying that these persons knew God but worshipped idols instead of God. To build his case, which he turns against judgmental Jews in chapter 2, he refers to typical practices of the fertility cults involving sex among priestesses and between men and eunuch prostitutes such as served Aphrodite at Corinth, from where he was writing this letter to the Romans. Their self-castration rites resulted in a bodily "penalty."

Lest one thinks this is just liberal semantics, note what Catherine Kroeger comments in the *Journal of the Evangelical Theological Society.* She says, in connection with this very text, that "Men wore veils and long hair as signs of their dedication to the god, while women used the unveiling and shorn hair to indicate their devotion. Men masqueraded as women, and in a rare vase painting from Corinth, a woman is dressed in satyr pants equipped with the male organ. Thus she dances before Dionysos, a deity who had been raised as a girl and was himself called male-female and "sham man."

Kroeger says further, "This was based on the sex exchange that characterized the cults of such great goddesses as Cybele (Aphrodite, Ishtar, etc.), the Syrian goddess, and Artemis of Epheses, and was more grisly. Males voluntarily castrated themselves and assumed women's garments. A relief from Rome shows a high priest of Cybele. The castrated priest wears veil, necklaces, earrings and feminine dress. He is considered to have exchanged his sexual identity and to have become a she-priest." As such, these religious prostitutes would engage in same-sex orgies in the pagan temples all along the coasts of Paul's missionary journeys.[45]

As Thielicke points out, "Paul's conception was one which was affected by the intellectual atmosphere surrounding the struggle with Greek paganism." However, when Paul gets to Romans 11:17 and 23, he explains that God goes beyond this law. Paul uses the very same concept, the same word, paraphusin, to express the idea that God is acting paraphusin in grafting the Gentiles as a branch onto the chosen people. People who were proclaimed by law in the Old Covenant to be unclean are seen as clean by God, accepted, and loved. Christianity teaches just the opposite of the law. How does one get homosexuality out of Gentiles becoming part of the faith? The writers used the same word, paraphusin.

This is a crucial teaching that impacts the argument that started in the 1200s concerning natural law. God has a way to supersede so-called natural law with love. Thus, "the true moral standard is not 'nature' but love," writes John Boswell.

Almost all commentators interpret Romans 1:13-3:20 as Paul's preliminary introduction to the next section of his writing. The point in this Scripture is that no unrighteous person is worthy to enter the Kingdom of Heaven, no matter what his or her particular brand of unrighteousness may be; and he is not referring to homosexuals although some have stretched it to include them. Romans 3:20 states clearly that no one is justified under the law. We only get there by the grace of God.

That brings us to the text that is relied upon as the exact statement needed to castigate homosexual people: I Cor. 6:9. Two Greek words here must be defined: *malakoi* and *arsenokoitai*.

Malakoi is not one of the 125 words in the Greek language that had to do with same-sex acts. We know exactly how the word was used based on the following examples.

- Xenophon uses the term for lazy men.[46]

- Epictetus shows the term refers to men who take life easy rather than enduring the hardships of philosophy.[47]

- Dionysius Halicarnassus wrote the same thing.[48]

- Dio Cassius, Plutarch, and Josephus, all, said malakoi are cowards.[49]

- Some 1200 years later, Thomas Aquinas wrongly applied it to masturbation[50] and so did Vincent of Beauvais.[51] Throughout ancient literature, malakoi are men who live lives of decadence and luxury. According to Josephus, a man may be accused of malakoi if he is weak in battle, enjoys luxury, or is reluctant to commit suicide.[52]

- Dio Chrysostom says that the common crowd might stupidly call a man malakos just because he studies a lot.[53]

- Aristotle defines malakoi precisely as unrestraint for anyone.[54]

- Plutarch referred to malakoi as passive sexuality in men.[55]

- Caelius Aurelianus (a late imperial physician) used it in referring to passive heterosexual men.[56]

Malakoi never had to do with same-sex acts or our term of homosexuality.

But take note of what the various translators have done to this text in I Corinthians 6:9 as they translate malakoi:

- Luther Weiehlinge: weakling, sissy

- King James: effeminate

- J.B. Phillips: effeminate, pervert

- Goodspeed: sensual, given to unnatural vice

- Jerusalem: German edition: sissies

- Jerusalem, English edition, 1966: Catamites, Sodomites

- Jerusalem, English edition, 1985: self-indulgent

- New American, Catholic, 1970: Sodomites

- New American, Catholic, 1987: boy prostitutes

- RSV (1946): sexual pervert

- RSV (1952): homosexuals, perverts

- New RSV 1989: male prostitutes

- Good News: homosexual perverts

- New English: homosexual perversion

In any event, the word "homosexual" did not apply when the Scriptures were written because there was no concept of homosexuality.

Arsenokoitai was also used in 1 Corinthians 6:9 to mean male prostitutes who service women. It never had anything to do with same-sex relationships.

Recent accurate translations, like the RSV (1989), have gone back to the original and correct use of the word.

97

1 Timothy 1:9-10 is another text used. The Greek word being translated is arsenokoitai. Male prostitute, as just noted, was its meaning even well into the fourth century. Even John Chrysostom, who hated same-sex acts, specifically used arsenokoitai to mean male prostitution.[57]

How ironic that some people, calling themselves "Christians" today, have fallen into the trap of using Scriptures like the scribes and Pharisees. They used Scripture to stone to death Stephen, had the very Son of God tortured to death on a cross, and had Paul jailed, beaten, and stoned. This strand of "Christians" certainly does not follow Jesus' teachings not to condemn. Rather, they follow the way of those who condemned Jesus. They betray Jesus.

Paul had been brought before the tribunal because the Jews were saying, "this man is persuading people to worship God contrary to the law" (Acts 18:12f). Furthermore, Acts 13:39 proclaims "...by him [Jesus] every one that believes is freed from everything from which you could not be freed by the law of Moses."

Note just some of what Paul had to say concerning the law in his letter to the Romans:

(2:14) Gentiles have not the law.

(3:20) No human is justified by works of the law.

(3:20-26) The righteousness of God has been manifested apart from the law...all have sinned and fallen short of the glory of God. They are justified by God's grace as a gift...he is justified who has faith in Jesus.

(3:28) We hold that one is justified by faith apart from the works of the law.

(4:14f) If it is the adherents of the law who are to be the heirs, faith is null and the promise void. For the law brings wrath, but where there is no law there is no transgression.

(6:14) For sin will have no dominion over you since you are not under the law but under grace.

(7:6) But now we are discharged from the law, dead to that which held us captive, so that we serve not under the old written code but in the new life of the Spirit.

(8:1) There is therefore now no condemnation for those who are in Christ Jesus. For the law of Life in Christ Jesus has set (us) free from the law of sin and death. For God has done what the law could not do.

(10:4) Christ is the end of the law.

(11:5) There is a remnant, chosen by grace, (11:6) but, if it is by grace, it is no longer on the basis of works, otherwise grace would no longer be grace.

(13:10) Love is the fulfilling of the law.

If Paul, who was educated in a very conservative rabbinical school, believed that God gave the law, there is no way he could have said the things he did about the law. Those who really believe that Christians can save themselves by obeying scriptural laws apparently have not read Acts 15 or 10:4; or any of Paul's writings, especially Romans and Galatians.

The Gospel according to John states, "To the Pharisees, Jesus said, 'You judge according to the flesh, I judge no one.'" This is the very opposite of how the Old Covenant worked through its 613 laws. In fact, the Old Covenant didn't work; that is why Jesus came into our world.

Many changes came when Jesus became flesh and stepped into history. He revealed a very different kind of relationship to God and to one another, the opposite from the way of the law, the way of the Pharisees.

As a result of the influence of the Gospel, a eunuch—whom the righteous of the day and the law considered one of the lowest outcasts—was the first person recorded to have been baptized. There is no way the eunuch could change what he was.

Robin Scroggs of Union Seminary states, "Biblical judgments against homosexuality are not relevant to today's debate. They should no longer be used; not because the Bible is not authoritative, but simply because it does not address the issues involved."

In studies of sex in history, Stanford classics professor John J. Winkler warns against "reading contemporary concerns and politics into texts and artifacts removed from their social context."

Victor Paul Furnish, SMU New Testament scholar and one of our General Conference Study Committee members, says, "There is no text on homosexual orientation in the Bible."

Alex Haiken, a Jew who believes that Jesus is the Messiah, wrote the following on a blog titled, "On Being Jewish, Christian, and Gay," (https://jewishchristiangay.wordpress.com/) on September 23, 2012.[58]

According to the book of James, we all make many mistakes. Perhaps nowhere is that propensity toward human error more obvious than in the history of biblical interpretation. One of the more interesting cases is that of John Calvin and Martin Luther, who were unanimous with the Catholic Church—and later the Protestant Church—in condemning the astronomer Nicolaus

Copernicus (1473-1543) as a heretic. What was Copernicus' crime? He asserted that the earth rotates around the sun. However, godly people, and the church, believed that the Bible taught otherwise. The proposition that the earth rotates around the sun was unacceptable to the Christian theologians of that period because there were many biblical passages that seemed to indicate that the earth did not move.

Among the texts frequently cited were the following: "He set the earth on its foundations; it can never be moved" (Psalms 104:5). "On the day the Lord gave the Amorites over to Israel, Joshua said to the Lord in the presence of Israel: 'O sun, stand still over Gibeon, O moon, over the Valley of Aijalon.' So the sun stood still, and the moon stopped, till the nation avenged itself on its enemies, as it is written in the Book of Jashar. The sun stopped in the middle of the sky and delayed going down about a full day" (Joshua 10:12-13). "Generations come and generations go, but the earth remains forever. The sun rises and the sun sets, and hurries back to where it rises" (Ecclesiastes 1:4-5). "The Lord reigns, he is robed in majesty; the Lord is robed in majesty and is armed with strength. The world is firmly established; it cannot be moved" (Psalm 93:1).

As far as Calvin and Luther were concerned, the Bible's words used to describe the sun rising and setting and moving across the sky could be interpreted to mean nothing other than that the sun, and not the earth, is the object that moves.

Martin Luther, referring to Joshua 10:13 in his series of Table Talks in 1539, said, "People gave ear to an upstart astrologer who strove to show that the earth revolves, not the heavens or the firmament, the sun and the moon. This fool wishes to reverse the entire science of astronomy; but sacred Scripture tells us that Joshua commanded the sun to stand still, and not the earth."

Luther's disciple Melanchthon, in emphasizing Ecclesiastes 1:4-5 said, "The eyes are witnesses that the heavens revolve in the space of 24 hours. But certain men, either from the love of novelty, or to make a display of ingenuity, have concluded that the earth moves; and they maintain that neither the eighth sphere nor the sun revolves... Now, it is a want of honesty and decency to assert such notions publicly, and the example is pernicious. It is the part of a good mind to accept the truth as revealed by God and to acquiesce in it."

And John Calvin, citing Psalm 93:1 in his Commentary on Genesis said, "Who will venture to place the authority of Copernicus above that of the Holy Spirit? ... the world also is established that it cannot be moved."

Calvin, Luther, and all believers with them took their stand on what they believed to be the clear teaching of Scripture and went to their graves condemning Copernicus as a heretic. It was many, many years before the church recognized that the descriptions of the sun's movement were what today any first-year Bible student calls "phenomenological" or merely descriptive. Allowance must be made, they discovered, especially in poetic texts, for the use of metaphorical language. Copernicus is only one such case in which the consensus of opinion about how the Bible should be understood has changed over the years. There are scores of others.

Although the Bible does not change, our understanding of how the biblical text should be interpreted has changed considerably. Throughout 2,000 years of church history, Christians of all traditions have used the Bible to support scores of doctrinal positions they believed to be as clear as mineral water but that they later had to admit were mistaken.

Over the years, Christians have found biblical "proof" that slavery is God-ordained; that women and blacks should not be allowed to vote; that interracial marriage is wrong; that women should not be allowed to preach, teach, or wear jewelry; that anti-Semitism is biblically supported; and on and on. As with the case of Copernicus, a number of biblical texts were cited to give support to each of these and, of course, all of the Bible verses that once footnoted these notions are still in the Bible.

As we look back over our 2,000 years of history, we find that oppression of one sort or another against people who are considered different—whether by means of race, color, gender, class, sexual orientation, or, as in the case of Copernicus, in the face of scientific or archeological discovery—has always been endemic. And to our great shame, the oppression and injustices are always carried out in the name of someone's Christianity. One of the lessons we can learn from these experiences is that reading and interpreting Scripture is not quite as simple as some would like to believe. A text does not simply "say what it says" despite the rational good intentions of some readers. For reading Scripture is not only a matter of what is written there, but also what we expect to find there, what we bring to the text, and what we take away from it. Reading Scripture, then, is by no means a clinical or a neutral affair.

The doctrine of those who read their anti-gay presuppositions into biblical texts is only the most recent doctrinal position that is well on the way to being generally acknowledged as an error. What would it take for those who still cling to their anti-gay doctrine to admit that they, like many well-intentioned Christians before them, have made a mistake? We would do well to remember that while it may seem evident to us that others did terrible things in the past, it isn't easy to see that we ourselves may be doing terrible things today.

To use Scripture to condemn homosexuality both misuses Scripture and denies the Gospel of Jesus Christ. We are back to what kind of meaning one gives to "the word of God" and the authority of the Bible.

Authority of the Bible

No consistent or unanimous answer has been given by the church to the question concerning the authority of Scripture, according to Herbert H. Farmer, a scholar who shared in writings included in the Interpreters Bible.[59] What we do have in Scripture is this: in 2 Timothy 3:16, written by Paul (who was first of all well educated in a conservative rabbinical school; second, converted to Christianity; and third, the most prolific writer of the New Covenant texts), the text states that the Scriptures are inspired by God and that they are profitable for teaching, for reproof, for correction and training in righteousness so that everyone who belongs to God may be proficient, equipped, for every good work. Why? Paul continues in 2 Timothy 4:3, "for the time is coming when people will not put up with sound doctrine but having itchy ears, they will accumulate for themselves teachers to suit their own desires and turn away from listening to the truth and wander away to myths."

The Scriptures are not treated as rules but as a guide for us in the correct way of living, and applying righteousness to every good work.

Profitable does not mean final or even a norm. Some use Scripture as a yardstick to measure by. But is it a yardstick or is it an inner principle that informs, grows, and matures amidst changes and challenges? Such a principle has no existence apart from the one to which it is relating. The norm for the Scripture is not like the yardstick, which is separate and outside of what it is measuring. That which guides us is an overall spirit as in a "family or community spirit" that takes the measure of the scripture to continue to create and foster.[60]

The normative relation of the Bible to one's faith and life is of the intrinsic kind. What the Bible says can be rightly interpreted only by those living the Christian way. For this life includes far more than ever could be contained in or expressed through a written record. Where the rubber meets the road is in whether we really believe in the incarnation, in God coming to us in the person of Jesus. Do we believe Acts 4:12 that "there is no other name under heaven given among men whereby we must be saved?" That "God so loved the world that he gave his only begotten son" (John 3:16) and "God was in Christ reconciling the world to himself" (2 Corinthians 5:19)?

These texts put the proper perspective on all that had been understood or recorded before. The former way was considered as a preparation for the new way. Why did Saul come to Jerusalem to persecute the Christians? Why was Stephan stoned to death? Why was Paul jailed, beaten, driven out of one town after another, again and again, and even stoned and left for dead? Why was someone as perfect as Jesus, the very son of God, tortured to death on a cross? It was very plain to most of the Jews that their religious way would end if Jesus' way succeeded. The new way was guided by love, not laws that lead to condemnation. The inspired writers of the old way wrote down their understandings of God, the holy other, relating to their needs. The records show a slow development of changing concepts: from polytheism to monotheism; from polygamy to monogamy; from marriage of relatives to marriage of those outside the family; from life continuing through progeny to the resurrection, etc.

The Christian way is expressed clearly in the teachings of Jesus: loving God and loving one's neighbor as oneself, caring for one's neighbor and living by grace. Jesus condemned no one and commanded his followers not to condemn anyone. We do not try to save ourselves by righteous living; rather, we live righteous lives because we have been saved by God. Righteous living shows itself in living love.

Chapter 6

Tradition

In this chapter, we will consider our Christology and the tradition of the church concerning sexuality. But as we do so, recall again and again through the flood story, the proclamations of the prophets (like Isaiah, Amos, Hosea, and Micah), and the exile in 587 that God was depicted as very upset with the way his people were living their lives. Their approach to God was not working. We also have noted that Jesus was very upset with the religious leaders who were not able to apply the law justly.

Jesus' teachings and Paul's writings make it very clear that we humans cannot save ourselves by any means, let alone a system of righteous living, like following certain laws. To believe that we can save ourselves is to assume the role of God. Salvation comes through God, not humans. It is only by God's grace that we are saved. It is blasphemous for us to even pretend to take on the role of God, the role of salvation. Setting up a system that results in being judgmental of one another presents the very problem that was presented in the story of

Adam and Eve in the Garden. The message from God had been very specific: we are not to eat the fruit of judgment.

Nevertheless, the very first thing the couple did after eating from the fruit of the tree was to be ashamed of each other's nakedness, their sexuality. Their conclusion was the very opposite of God's perspective. The two stories of creation tell us that they were naked and God was very pleased with the results of his creation. Man sees things not only differently from God, but in a biased way. The scriptures and church history have showed us—from the Garden story through today—the problems created when we try to play God. Neither fig leaves nor church doctrine can cover our decisions to contradict God's way.

One of the most important learnings about Jesus is that he came into the world, "not to condemn the world, but that he might save the world."[61] Why this kind of contrast—condemnation versus saving? He told us specifically not to condemn others.[62] We will be judged the same way we judge others. God justifies, so how can any take it upon themselves to judge others?[63] When a woman caught in adultery was brought before Jesus,[64] the accusers quoted Moses' law to him, that she should be stoned to death.[65] This law stated that both the man and the woman should be stoned to death. Why was just the woman brought to him? Where was the man? If she was caught in the act, a man must have been present. These men who brought this woman wanted to hear what Jesus had to say about the incident. His response was, "Let him who is without sin cast the first stone." They all dropped their stones and left her standing there. Jesus said to her, "Neither do I condemn you." Paul reminds us that beginning with Adam, throughout history all have sinned.[66] He goes on to say that now, with the coming of Jesus, all are justified, saved. For Jesus, judgment and condemnation had no part in healing or salvation. Jesus' concern was salvation, not condemnation. Both the concepts of healing and salvation come out of the common root having to do with wholeness. Paul goes on to tell us that when we are guided by Jesus, we are not condemned; rather, we are saved by grace.[67]

Since every single one of us is a sinner, we are not capable of saving ourselves no matter what we do to rectify the sin. Jesus tried to teach us to turn in a new direction, toward God; to have a purpose that guides us from within, a purpose guided by the love of God. But here again comes another problem for us because of the way this concept is translated. All too often, the translators turn to a French-based word to try to get at the meaning of the Greek word used, *metanomia*. That French word is "repentance." The French word repentance is colored by the fact that many people read it as "being sorry for." Metanomia means simply to turn and go in a new direction. Merely being sorry for what we have done does not bring salvation if that is all we do; we still need to go in a very different direction from the one in which we have been living. One can live the rest of one's life being sorry but never do anything to make a difference. In either case, it is not in our power to save ourselves. Rather, we are saved by the grace of God. And it is by grace we should share our lives with others. "They will know we are Christians by our love." We are to forgive. We are to reconcile. We are to be good neighbors, even loving those who hate us, to the extent of even loving our enemies. That is Jesus' teaching, Jesus' way.

I can imagine nothing worse than the terrible torture Jesus was put through on the cross, yet his prayer, while suffering and dying, was, "Father, forgive them, for they know not what they do." If this is not a contrast between the old way and the new, what is?

Hebrews 5, 6, and 7 try to show the difference. These chapters tell us that Christ is of the order of Melchizedek. What we know from the Ugaritic texts, Psalms 76 and 100, and Genesis 14 is that Melchizedek means "My god is Righteousness." Zedek was the Ugarit god whose name meant "righteous." Melchizedek was the King of Salem (Peace), which later became Jeru-salem. Not only was Melchizedek king, he was the high priest of the god Zedek. What the author of Hebrews is pointing out is that this way of peace and righteousness preceded the priestly orders of Aaron and the Levitical priests. The very first—and more important—covenant with God was through faithfulness, not by following laws. Jesus came representing living by grace in contrast to the way of Moses and the Law.

The Jewish leaders certainly understood this. That is why they reacted they way they did: the crucifixion of Jesus, Saul persecuting the Christians, the stoning to death of Stephen, then the jailings and beatings of Paul, etc. These actions all demonstrate specifically that the Jewish leaders saw that what Christians were doing was changing the way of the law. The followers of Jesus certainly understood this, also, and went so far as to reject practically all the laws of the Old Covenant at the first Church Council held in Jerusalem in about 49 AD, as we see recorded in Acts 15.

That very first Church Council[68] concluded that none of the Old Testament laws applied to Christians except for four, all of which had to do with idol or fertility cult worship. Paul confirms this decision as he tells us again and again that the law no longer applies.[69] "Those who have Christ do not have the law." Yet, many people calling themselves Christians today put more emphasis on those Old Covenant laws than on Christ's teachings. Worse still, they try to apply New Covenant teachings like laws of old, causing the same problems of judgment and condemnation. Our concern here is, throughout history, how has the church connected scripture, especially Jesus' teachings, to the issue of same-sex relationships?

I have heard people who call themselves Christian claim that the church has "always been against homosexuality." As we take a quick trip through our church history, you will note that I do not use the term homosexuality. I am not using that term because it did not exist until 1869. It never got into any Bible until 1952. In 1989, that Bible, the RSV, went back to the original, true meaning. Those texts do not necessarily mean homosexual, as we shall note later on. The RSV no longer uses the word "homosexual." I will use the term "same-sex relationships" or "gay."

Have there been those who have spoken out against gay or same-sex relationships? Yes. John Chrysostom, Peter Damian, and Thomas Aquinas were some of the few. Interestingly, no one used the scriptures as authority against same-sex relationships until about the 13th Century.

Many pagan writers (AD 56-117) objected to Christianity precisely because of what they claimed was "sexual looseness" on the part of its adherents, and much Christian apologetic at the time was aimed at defending Christians against the common belief that they were given to every form of sexual indulgence—including same-sex acts.[70]

Origen, who lived from AD 184-253, is known as the first Christian theologian. He was so convinced that sex was bad that he castrated himself. The mood of the church was so changeable concerning him that he went from anathema (an outcast of the church) to being a saint. Although he was deeply loved at first, he fell out of favor and was pronounced anathema because of his belief in the preexistence of souls and in universal salvation. Eventually, he was made a saint. Origen was an early Christian Alexandrian scholar and theologian, and one of the most distinguished writers of the early church. Today he is regarded as one of the church fathers. Nevertheless, he laid the foundation for looking down on sex—not same-sex acts, but all sex.

As noted above, Origen believed souls existed before entering man and also in universal salvation. It is believed that Origen based his universal salvation concepts on Romans 7:12-25, where Paul explains his struggle with sin. By this example, he shows that sin is in all of us, no matter what we know and will.

Furthermore, Origen believed that sex passed on sin from one generation to another. He was so convinced of this that he castrated himself to guarantee that his sperm would not be misused to pass on sin. However, this concept had nothing to do with a proper reading of any Scripture. It was purely Origen's theory. His idea was that all sex is bad because it transfers sin to the next generation.

Next, there was Augustine. Augustine of Hippo was Bishop of Hippo Regius (present day Annaba, Algeria). By his own admission, he was extremely promiscuous prior to his conversion to Christianity. Perhaps it was the teaching of Origen that made him feel guilty about his promiscuity. Augustine came up with the theory of original sin. He believed that because Adam and Eve sinned, sin is passed on through sex. According to him, it is bad enough that sex has to be used to continue the human race; any other use of sex is even worse. It certainly should not be used for enjoyment, even and especially with one's spouse.

The irony behind his theory is the fact that sex had been seen not only as good, but connected with the holy for some 2,000 years! Adam and Eve's sin was not connected with sex but with trying to be like God in eating from the tree of the knowledge of good and evil. Nor was it Adam and Eve who were cursed after committing the sin, but the ground. Read the story in Genesis 3 for yourself. As a result, God changed the order of things so that now the serpent would have to crawl, the woman would have a more painful childbirth, and man would have to till the soil for a living. The sin was in their decision making. Sex had absolutely nothing to do with it. Augustine's conclusion, resulting in his concepts of the fall of man and doctrine of original sin, had nothing to do with a proper understanding of the Scriptures.

It is crucial to understand that where spokespersons were against gay sexuality later on, they also, categorically, rejected human erotic experience—including between husband and wife. Ironically, Augustine himself admitted that no married persons of his acquaintance engaged in intercourse solely for the purpose of procreation.[71] Nowhere does the

Bible teach this concept. Augustine's view is the very opposite of the Scriptures' teaching of God's view, as the creation stories plainly reveal. God saw their nakedness and called it very good. As Paul said, it was their behavior, being judgmental, that was the problem.

Ironically, Augustine created a doctrine to judge everyone and the results were similar to what happened because of the Mosaic laws for righteous living. The acceptance of Augustine's concept of sex as bad and transmitting sin has plagued the church and Christians to this day. Our present day problems concerning sexuality started with Origen and Augustine.

Logic tells us, if sin is inherited, then man has no choice about sinning; therefore, how can he be considered guilty of sinning if the behavior is naturally inherited? It is a ridiculous doctrine. As a result of this doctrine, in the 4th century there were instances, in the West, of canonical enactment of penalties for members of the clergy who did not observe abstinence from sex. The earliest known is that of the Council of Elvira (c. 306): bishops, presbyters, deacons, and others with a position in the ministry were to abstain completely from sexual intercourse with their wives and from the procreation of children. According to the Council of Elvira, "If anyone disobeys, he shall be removed from the clerical office."

Sometime between 387 and 400, the Council of Carthage decreed that bishops, priests and deacons abstain from conjugal intercourse with their wives, so that those who served at the altar would keep a perfect chastity. At the same time, same-sex prostitution was not only tolerated, but actually taxed by Christian emperors in eastern cities during the 300s and 400s when Christianity became the state religion.[72] Even Saint John Chrysostom, who hated same-sex behavior, admitted that gay sexuality was absolutely rampant in Christian society of fourth- century Antioch, from the highest level on down.[73]

Ausonius, a Christian contemporary of Chrysostom in the late 300s, had volumes of gay literature that he translated from Greek to Latin. He was passionately loved by Saint Paulinus, Bishop of Nola. Their relationship was put into poetry and set the tone for much of the love literature of medieval Europe.[74]

Chrysostom spoke out against gay sexuality. However, his arguments were not based on Scripture but on Manichean philosophy and his concept of man being belittled if he took the role of an inferior woman.[75] However, the church took no action on Chrysostom's complaints. Plutarch argued just the opposite—that sexual desire amongst heterosexuals was a consequence of sin.[76]

The arguments of Augustine, Jerome, and Origen were basically against eroticism, which they saw as taking pleasure in sex. They believed pleasure should be divorced from sex, that sex was only for procreation.[77] "A man who loves his wife too much is an adulterer," wrote Vincent of Beavais.[78] This is the philosophy that caused many Christian ascetics to view heterosexuality as "The chief danger to the soul."[79] In their view, sex was only for procreation.

Although Christianity had been the state religion for two centuries by 533, there was no Empire legislation against same-sex behavior until that time, and then only temporarily. That legislation was not by the church. The only persons known to have been punished as a result of those laws were prominent bishops: Isaiah of Rhodes, the prefecture (magistrate or governor) of Constantinople; and Alexander of Diospolis of Thrace. Again, this law did not come from the church, but was enacted by Justinian in a political move.[80] Procopius of Caesarea, a contemporary historian of the time, states specifically that Justinian did this because the bishops were part of a wealthy opposing faction called the Greens, and Justinian did not concern himself with offenses committed after the passage of the laws. It was politics, not Christian values.[81]

When Justinian's wife, Theodora (of the Blue Party), had a young man (a Green) dragged from church to convict him for gay sex, many prominent people came to his aid and the judge refused to hear the charges. Theodora had bribed witnesses and tortured one of the young man's friends to have them witness against him. The whole city celebrated a holiday in his honor when he was set free.[82] The fact is, almost without exception, the few laws against same-sex behavior that were passed before the 13th century were enacted by civil authorities without advice or support from the church. Furthermore, these laws were frequently aimed at the clergy.[83]

In Visigothic Spain (500s-600s), the church held out for 40 years and through six national church councils against cooperation with the Visigothic laws against gay sex. Finally, under direct orders from the monarchy to enact ecclesiastical legislation, the church did issue a conciliar decree stipulating degradation from holy orders and exile for clerics convicted of same-sex behavior.[84]

When Leo became Bishop of Rome in 545, he insisted upon being made pope, the bishop over all bishops, the "daddy" or "Pappa" of the church. To support this idea, he had a committee trace a line of bishops back to Peter for a line of succession and used the text in Matthew 16:18-19 as authority for this kind of position. The text had been mistranslated into the Latin version. The assumption for the establishment of a pope and the church having this kind of authority was all based on Jesus' use of the word "rock" in Matthew 16. Leo claimed that Jesus referred to Peter as the foundation on which the church was to be built.

Even our English translation does not give us the proper meaning of this text. Greek, like German and French, has masculine, feminine, and neuter word endings. When Jesus referred to Peter as a "rock," he used, of course, *petros*, the masculine form meaning rock. However, when he referred to the rock on which the church was built, he used *petra*, the feminine form. If he had meant Peter, the word "rock" would have remained masculine. He was referring to Peter's statement of faith as the foundation of the church, not Peter himself. Furthermore, if Jesus had meant authority for Peter alone, he would not have used the same authority for all the disciples as he did in Matthew 18:18. Peter was not specially selected. At that point in history (545), the church, by way of the pope, took on authority above that of the writings or Scripture. After all, there would be no authorized Bible for many centuries yet.

Some like to refer to Pope Saint Gregory III (690-741) and the specified penances that he listed: 160 days for lesbian activities and as little as one year for same-sex acts between males. They neglect to mention that the penance for priests going hunting was three years—a far worse sin.[85]

Charlemagne (late 700s-early 800s) was shocked to discover that some of the monks were "sodomites" as he put it. He thought that a life of chastity would preclude this. At that time, sodomy referred to any emission of semen not directed exclusively toward the procreation of a legitimate child within matrimony, and the term included much—if not most—heterosexual activity. However, no legislation was enacted against this activity.[86]

By the ninth century, almost every area of Europe had some sort of local code. Although sexuality occupied a considerable portion of such legislation and Christian teachings regarding rape, adultery, incest, illegitimacy, marriage, fornication, etc., received the sanctions of the civil authorities that promulgated the codes, same-sex relations are not proscribed in any of them.[87] The fourth Addito by Benedict Levita, which purports to show that Charlemagne (768-814) acted against gays, has been found to be "an invention" by Benedict. It was not true.[88] In 829, The Council of Paris specifically prohibited priests from referring to penitentials for penances for same-sex acts.[89]

As stated before, sodomy has had different meanings through the centuries. In biblical times, it had to do with being inhospitable, as Jesus himself noted. In the Middle Ages, it referred to any emission of semen not directed exclusively toward the procreation of a legitimate child within matrimony, and the term included much, if not most, heterosexual activity. Saint Boniface referred exactly to this when writing of people in England who rejected marriage and lived in adultery.[90]

Hincmar of Reims (845) used the word sodomy in the same way as he referred to any sexual release of semen: with a nun, a relative, the wife of a relative, a married woman, any woman in any way which precluded conception—or by oneself. He wrote, "Therefore let no one claim he has not committed sodomy if he has acted contrary to nature with either man or woman or has deliberately and consciously defiled himself by rubbing, touching or other improper actions." He saw the human seed as impure.[91]

In the early 900s, Caesar of Prum noted that the punishment for anal intercourse was gender blind. It was the act, not the parties involved. The penalty was the same for a married couple as for two males, and it was no more severe than penalty for any heterosexual fornication.[92]

And Burchard, bishop of Worms, who died in 1025, saw gay sex as a variety of fornication but less serious than comparable heterosexual activity.[93] During the 10th and 12th centuries, the population of European cities increased by as much as 800 percent. All kinds of free and democratic ideas flourished and more people became interested in travel, learning, and the classics. Ovid, Virgil, and Plato were read and gay sentiments were respected. In the church, two movements began towards gay people. A small, vociferous group of ascetics referred to Chrysostom's hostility to same-sex acts and compared these acts to murder. They struggled to change both public and theological opinion against these acts. The majority of the church turned a deaf ear to the anti-gays. This majority movement within the church asserted a positive value of same-sex relations and celebrated them in an outburst of Christian gay literature that is still without parallel in the Western world.

Peter Damian was outspoken against gays and quoted the Council of Ancyra (314) as a support for his feelings, claiming it legislated against same sex behavior, which was false. It did not.[94] Pope Saint Leo IX (1002-1054) sent a polite acknowledgment to Damian, assuring him that he had demonstrated himself to be an enemy of carnal pollution. However, Leo declined to accede to Damian's demands that all clergy guilty of any sort of same-sex offense be removed from office and decided that only those most severely sinful might be degraded from their rank.[95] The Lateran Synod (1059) issued a series of canons in response to Damian's concerns but not one of them on same-sex relations.[96] Following this, Pope Alexander II (1061-1073, Anselm of Lucca), an ardent and determined reformer of clerical mores, actually stole Damian's "Liber Gomorrhianus" and locked it up.[97]

Fifty years later, a prominent churchman, Ivo of Chartres, failed to get Pope Urban II to react to well known, high-ranking prelates involved in same-sex activities. These prelates included Ralph, the archbishop of Tours; John, the bishop of Orleans; Ralph's brother, the former bishop of Orleans; and the King himself. Even though Pope Urban disliked Ralph for siding with King Philip of France against the papal legate, Hugh, he would not agree to take action against them. Ralph's lover was consecrated on March 1, 1098.[98] The same-sex activities of Archbishop Ralph were widely known and popular songs were written about him and his life. John of Orleans ruled long and effectively as bishop, retiring with honor some 40 years later.[99] Pope Paschal II intervened directly to depose a known adulterer from a French bishopric only four years later, while both Ralph and John remained in office.[100]

In 1102, the Council of London took measures to inform the public that, in the future, sodomy must be confessed as a sin. As a result of this action, Saint Anselm, the archbishop of Canterbury, in a letter to the Archdeacon William, prohibited the publication of the decree, saying, "This sin has hitherto been so public that hardly anyone is embarrassed by it."[101] This prohibition would also have violated the papal decree by Pope Leo IX, forbidding extreme measures of any sort in dealing with same-sex relations among the clergy.[102] It was also during the reign of Pope Leo IX (1049-1054) that the First Lateran Council declared all clergy marriages invalid. "It was during these 200 years that unparalleled spiritual reform took place within the church so it can hardly be argued that indifference to gay sexuality was simply the consequence of apathy."[103]

Gay sex was so common amongst the clergy that the mere fact of having taken orders seems to have rendered one liable to the suspicion of being a "sodomite." An astounding amount of gay literature was written during this time, basically from the pens of the clerics. This same period witnessed the effort to formulate a theology that could incorporate expressions of gay feelings into the most revered Christian lifestyle, monasticism. Saint Anselm, the most prominent and imposing intellectual figure of his day, brought the tradition of passionate friendship among monks into the limelight.[104]

Many 12th-century clerics, monastic and secular, were involved and wrote about passionate friendships like Anselm's, such as Saint Aelred of Rievauex and Saint Bernard of Clairvaux. The approach to sexuality adopted by 12th-century theologians effectively decriminalized gay sex relations altogether. When Peter Lomvard, writing at the height of positive attitudes toward gay people, composed what was to become the standard moral text for all of Europe's Catholic universities for the next century, he made no mention whatsoever of gay sexuality. "The sin against nature" is discussed in his extensive section dealing with marriage and adultery and is defined as the illicit use of a woman by a man, with reference to Augtustine's curious principle that such actions were more reprehensible between husband and wife than between a married man and a prostitute."[105]

From the later 12th through the 14th centuries, there was a quest for intellectual and institutional uniformity. This resulted in consolidating and strengthening civil and ecclesiastical power and administrative organization. Theology began to be organized into systematic formulas. The Inquisition developed to enforce theological concepts and get rid of divergent opinions. Secular and ecclesiastical concerns were melded in the interest of uniformity. Collections of canon law were joined to Roman civil law and Christian religious principles to standardize clerical supervision of ethical, moral, and legal problems. An astronomical increase in legislation developed, to the extent of some 100 volumes!

This consolidation of power brought about loss of freedom for minority groups: women, the poor, Jews, and Muslims. Intolerance increased. Lepers were prosecuted and imprisoned. Widespread fears developed concerning anyone who was different from the majority. Those who were different were seen as alien and disruptive to the social order. Organizing the Crusades roused to fervor feelings against the enemies of Christendom and participants couldn't wait to express their hostility. They showed less and less discrimination about whom they might attack. On the way to the Holy Land, the first crusade got no further than Germany where the Jews there were attacked and slaughtered by the thousands. Christians who had sexual relations with Jews were equated with those who had intercourse with animals.[106]

The Fourth Lateran Council (1215) forbade Jews to hold any public office, restricted their financial arrangements, prohibited them from going outdoors during the last days of Holy Week, and ordered them to wear clothing that distinguished them from Christians.[107] The poor were increasingly seen as members of an alien element rather than the victims of circumstance and this reached such a pitch that the papacy forbade overly zealous adherence to the ancient ideal of apostolic poverty as heretical![108] Laymen who lent at interest were excommunicated and denied Christian burial.[109] It was this kind of social-ecclesiastical setting that began to see gays as different, alien, even the enemy.

In such an atmosphere, it is scarcely surprising that gay people became objects for attack. The first record of attacking them was Morlaiz's *Contempt of the World*. It claimed that same-sex acts were symptoms of hedonism and sensuality, like heterosexual fornication, greed, venality, and the arrogance of the wealthy.[110]

For the first time, against theological precedent, Peter Cantor (d. 1197) connected Romans 1:26-27 with sodomy. He argued that it was not merely a violation of chastity but on a par with murder. He invoked the Law of Leviticus as precedent for physical punishment although it had been treated as allegorical and ignored by most writers since the Council of Jerusalem (AD 49). Cantor was distressed that there were no ecclesiastical sanctions against this kind of behavior.[111]

Because of the kind of social flux and Cantor's urging, Lateran III of 1179 became the first church council to rule on same-sex acts (the literal interpretation referred to all non-procreative intercourse). This was more than 1000 years after Christianity began. At the same time, Lateran III imposed sanctions against money lenders, heretics, Jews, Muslims, mercenaries, and others.[112] Since this rule of the Third Lateran Council was not widely accepted or enforced, the Fourth Lateran Council (1215) retreated somewhat regarding gay people, although it passed even more stringent legislation regarding Jews, Muslims, and other minorities. Laity were not mentioned at all—this was only in connection with clerical celibacy.[113]

"The earliest and most drastic legislation against gay people enacted by any government of the High Middle Ages was passed in the nascent kingdom of Jerusalem by Europeans attempting to create a western feudal society in the Muslim Middle East. These laws were drafted only decades after the first crusade."[114] To rouse European antagonism against gays, it was charged that Christians were cooperating in beautifying and selling hapless Christian youth to Saracens for their evil sexual purposes.[115] With such suspicion at work, even the orthodoxy of Saint Thomas Aquinas came under a cloud.[116]

It was in the 13th century that connecting same-sex acts to nature began.[117] "Between 1250 and 1300, gay activity passed from being completely legal in most of Europe to incurring the death penalty."[118] But very little is known about the actual application of the death penalty for any crimes. Despite all this, there is little noticeable change in actual church practice throughout the 13th century.[119] *The Book of*

Excommunication written by French cardinal Berenger Fredol at the end of the 13th century does not even mention gay acts.[120]

As southern Europe became more and more urban and cultural centers more removed from daily contact with agricultural lifestyles, "nature" came to seem a more and more important and benevolent force and increasingly preoccupied Christian thought.[121] Many writers began using examples of animals as "natural" lessons for humans. Peter Damian (1007-1072) wrote, "From animals people may learn what behavior should be imitated, what avoided."[122] However, no reason is given as to why this might be so. Although the weasel (labeled a reptile) receives more or less favorable treatment in Damian's letter, the hyena's sex changes earn it degradation as a "dirty animal" whose example should be avoided by all Christians.[123]

During this time, a very popular book was written, *The Dreams of Arisleus*. The hero is transported in a dream to a land where the natives practice exclusive same-sex behavior. Arisleus informs the country's king that such unions will not produce offspring but will always be sterile, and that only male-female unions will be fruitful. The confusion of moral and "natural" laws in the work is striking. Arisleus urges the King to abandon same-sex behavior in favor of incest, which will be more productive, and counters the king's objections to incest with the biblical example of Adam's children, believing that since that family consisted of the only human beings that the children had to mate to grow the race.[124] How is that for scriptural exegesis?

Ah, the wonders of the misuse of scripture! But a curious paradox developed. With the revival of Augustine's Manichean animal philosophy that certain animals were innately seen as participating in same-sex activity, there was also the contrary idea: that the absence of such behavior among animals constituted proof of its "unnaturalness." The successful coexistence of these opposing ideas is evidence of the ability of the human mind to entertain paradoxes with equanimity. "Within the same 30 lines of poetry, Bernard of Morlaix castigated gay people for imitating hyenas, and for indulging in behavior unknown to animals."[125] Apparently, not all forms of logic are the same. Apparently, hyenas are not animals in this case.

And, in Vincent of Beauvais's *Speculum doctrinale*, the argument that animals do not practice same-sex behavior is followed immediately by the accusation that men who indulge in such acts are like hares.[126]

No specifically Christian theology informs Alain de Lille's *The Complaint of Nature*. The arguments are theistic but entirely philosophical. Nothing so charmed the tastes of the age as non-Christian proofs of Christian moral principles, and the pagan figure of Natura employed by de Lille and others provided just such reinforcement for those who wished to denigrate same-sex activity.[127] Throughout the 12th and 13th centuries, the goddess Natura gained in stature and familiarity.[128] The popular acceptance of the goddess Natura as the champion of heterosexual fecundity already had a profound impact on the development of moral theology in the 13th century. By a strange irony, a popular literary figure of decidedly pagan origin speaking on her own authority for the sexual preferences of the majority had come to dominate even dogmatic theology.[129]

Nevertheless, it was not until the 13th century that actual definitions of "nature" were formulated to exclude same-sex activity. This means of removing gay sexuality from the realm of the natural presupposes something few subsequent theologians were willing to admit: that Christian society equates the good with the common. Although this was true to a certain extent, it was not a position the church wished to accept. After all, Aristotle was convincing most scholars at that time that mere statistical deviance could not be held sinful, since "heroic virtue," sainthood, superior intellect, and even sexual continence were statistically deviant. Certainly, celibate clergy would be "unnatural."[130]

Albertus Magnus was the first to synthesize this with grace and reason. In his *Summa Theologiae*, he condemned same-sex acts as the gravest type of sexual sins because they offended "grace, reason, and nature." He never gave any explanation as to why this was so but he did relate it to Romans 1:26-27.[131] However, to make it even more confusing, in other writings, Magnus spoke of same-sex behavior as a contagious disease passed from person to person, especially common among the wealthy, and that it was innate (inborn).[132] Ironically, Magnus had a cure, a relatively easy cure that was used for other illnesses in Arabia: take fur from the neck of an Arabian animal he called *alzabo*, burn it with pitch and grind it to a fine powder, then apply it to the "sodomite's" anus. He was ignorant of the fact that alzabo was the Latin translation of the Arabic *al-dabc*, which means hyena, the very animal that was anathema![133] What kind of logic is this?

Magnus's most famous pupil was Saint Thomas Aquinas (d. 1274). Aquinas's *Summa Theologiae* became a standard for orthodox opinion right up until the present and permanently established the concept of "natural" as the touchstone of Roman Catholic ethics, although his writings were controversial during his lifetime and for some time thereafter. Understanding how Aquinas's attitudes about same-sex behavior could fit in any way with his general moral principles is a paradox. Despite his absolute conviction in every other context that humans were morally and intellectually superior to animals and therefore not only permitted but obliged to engage in many types of activity unknown or impossible to lower beings, Aquinas resorted again and again to animal behavior as the final arbiter in matters of human sexuality, falsely believing that animals did not have same-sex relationships.

Promiscuity (fornication), of course, was common among familiar animals, like dogs and cats—so common, in fact, that even the most devoted compared humans given to obsessive or wanton venereal pursuits to animals. If animals could naturally pursue lives of such carefree and expansive sexuality, why could not humans naturally do likewise? So it was that Aquinas argued both sides of the issue in condemning promiscuity.[134]

Indeed, Aquinas conceded, heterosexual promiscuity would be no more serious than gluttony if it were not for its potentially harmful effects. Although one excessive meal has no permanent consequences, a single act of heterosexual fornication could ruin the life of a human being: that of the illegitimate and uncared for child produced.[135] Following that logic, one would surmise that same-sex behavior would not be as bad because no illegitimate child could result. So Aquinas switches to the argument that the semen is not used for the purpose of procreation, therefore, gay sex is unnatural—contrary to nature—hence sinful, since the design of nature represented the will of God.

However, even Aquinas, unlike later writers, realized that this argument had fatal flaws. He himself raised the question of other "misuses" of nature's design. Is it sinful for a man to walk on his hands, when nature has clearly designed feet for this purpose? Such questions can go on and on. So, again Aquinas shifts, focusing not on the misuse of the organs involved, but the fact that through the act in question, the propagation of the human species was impeded.[136] This line of reasoning was based on the ethical premise that the physical increase of the human species constitutes a moral good, which bore no relation to any New Testament or early Christian authority and which had been specifically rejected by Saint Augustine. Moreover, this argument contradicted Aquinas's own teachings. Nocturnal emissions impede the increase of the human race in precisely the same way as same-sex activity (i.e., by expending semen to no creative purpose), yet Aquinas not only considered them inherently sinless but the result of natural causes. Again, the wonders of logic!

Furthermore, voluntary virginity, which Aquinas and others considered the crowning Christian virtue, so clearly operated to the detriment of the species in this regard that he very specifically argued in its defense that individual humans are not obliged to contribute to the increase or preservation of the species through procreation! This was written in this same treatise.[137]

In the end, Aquinas admitted that his categorization of same-sex acts as unnatural was a concession to popular sentiment and parlance. Since sins are unnatural, by theological definition, same-sex acts would have to be shown to be sinful apart from their "unnaturalness." They would have to be immoral from a theological point of view. Aquinas further admitted that "same sex desire was the result of a 'natural' condition," which would logically have made behavior resulting from it not only inculpable, but "good." And that is a direct quote.[138]

Saint Thomas Aquinas does not cite the Bible in all of his reasoning against same-sex acts. In fact, in his commentary on Romans 1, he relates it to temple prostitution! In his commentary on 1 Corinthians 6:9, he refers to "catamites."[139] It is these ethics of the 13th century that formulated the decision making behind the concepts that some follow today against homosexuality.

If we are going to use the ethical system of the 13th century, we should not forget that society took an even more powerful moral stand against usury than toward gay sexuality. Many more biblical passages were claimed to relate to usury. Natural law forbade it. By the 14th century, usury incurred more severe penalties in church law than "sodomy."[137] But today, usury is the god of capitalism. Both are condemned by the same dogma, yet today one is considered good and the other bad. If you are confused by this kind of thinking about ethics, you have every right to be.

Church history shows clearly that, for the first 1300 years, the church supported same-sex relationships. It was not the use of scriptures that began the condemnation of same sex relationships. Instead, the practice of condemnation began from Manichean philosophy, falsehoods about animals, and a false application of so-called natural law.

However, if one believes in natural law, then one should be aware of very important information about homosexuals. Because of new technology and a closer study of hormones and their relationships to reproductive and sexual functioning, we have more exact information than has ever been available to us before. These precise studies are showing impacts by different hormonal quantities on embryological development that predispose particular patterns of sexual behavior. And even Thomas Aquinas stated in his *Summa Theologea* that if same-sex acts were proven to be natural, there would be no wrong in them. We will look at this more closely later.

From the time of Thomas Aquinas's natural law, no changes to speak of addressed the issue of same-sex relationships until 1869, when the concept of homosexuality developed. More than 80 years later, in 1952, the word "homosexual" was entered into the scriptures, and now, people believe it was in the scriptures from the beginning. It was not. As I stated before, the translation began using the word "homosexual" in 1952, the RSV, changed back to the correct translation in 1989 and since then.

Concerning this topic, Brawley, a Baptist theologian, says, "Nor can any responsible Christian—after the revolutionary changes in Christian thought in the past 20 years, much less in the past 300—maintain that Christian interpretations are those conforming to Christian tradition. The traditions, all of them, have changed too much and are far too open to cynical manipulation to be taken as foundations for gauging the ethical value of a reading of Scripture."[140]

The Bible has been used authoritatively in a different way since the Council of Trent in 1546. Remember, technically, we did not have a Bible until then.

I hope that all of the above, in the chapters on experience, Scripture, and tradition, form a firmer foundation to build on as we look to reason in chapter seven.

Chapter 7

Reason

As we bring together these backgrounds of Scripture, tradition, and experience, let us now consider reason in making a decision about the issue of homosexuality. But first, what is the scientific truth about homosexuality?

The following information can help clarify what homosexuality is and how people become that way. First, let us face the fact that homosexuals do not prefer to be homosexual any more than heterosexuals prefer to be heterosexuals. "Sexual preference" is a moral and political term, not a factual term. It implies voluntary choice, which is not so. The concept of voluntary choice about one's sexuality is as much in error as one choosing to have brown hair or to be right or left handed.[141]

Biological Background

The origins of a person being exclusively homosexual or exclusively heterosexual must address primarily the genesis of bisexuality.

Monosexuality, whether homosexual or heterosexual, is secondary and a derivative of the primary bisexual or ambisexual potential. Ambisexuality has its origins in evolutionary biology and in embryology of sexual differentiation. Or, to put it another way, the fetus in the first trimester is both male and female and is ready to be either bisexual or monosexual. If monosexual, it will be either homosexual or heterosexual.

This information has been known for some 70 years. The fetus is sexually bipotential. According to Dr. John Money of Johns Hopkins University, "Thereafter, if the fetal testes do not start producing the needed hormones at the end of the first trimester, the fetus will become female. Sexual differentiation proceeds to be that of a female unless masculinization hormones are added."[142] Masters and Johnson tell us, "Investigative endocrinologists have been aided by technological advances such as radioimmunoassay techniques, which for the first time have permitted precise quantification of various hormones related to reproduction and sexual functioning."[143]

Studies have verified this again and again starting in 1940. Not just the body, but the brain also has both sexes present and these pathways in the brain need modification during the development of the forming of sexuality. The internal genitalia also have both sexes present. Having both sexes present allows for the possible coexistence of both masculine and feminine nuclei and pathways, and the behavior they govern. The two need not necessarily have equality. One may be more dominant than the other. The external genitalia have only one sex present but it can be modified.[144]

The occurrence of androgen deficiency, androgen being a hormone developed in the testes to stimulate development of male sex characteristics in genetic male fetuses, or of androgen excess in genetic female fetuses during the critical period when the brain is differentiated, can predispose these individuals to the development of homosexuality.[145]

Psychoneuroendocrinology has verified that both heterosexuality and homosexuality are understood as two expressions of monosexuality, as opposed to bisexuality. Sexual status (or orientation) is assimilated and locked into the brain as bisexual, monosexually homosexual, or monosexually heterosexual.[146]

According to Masters and Johnson, "One of the two masculinizing hormones from the fetal testes is actually a defeminizing hormone. It is called MIH (mullerian inhibiting hormone). It has a brief life span during which it vestigiates (or withers away) the two mullerian ducts and prevents them from developing into a uterus and fallopian tubes (oviducts). The other hormone masculinizes. It is testosterone (or one of the metabolites, which is a metabolic result that is necessary for another process) and it presides over the two wolffian ducts (ducts of this embryonic stage persisting as a functional ureter in females and as a urinogenital duct in males) and directs their development into the male internal accessory organs, including the prostate gland and seminal vesicals."[147]

Differentiation of the internal genitalia is ambitypic (having both sex tissues), conforming to both male and female. That is, the basis or foundation for both the male and female are present to begin with, after which one set vestigiates while the other set proliferates. By contrast, differentiation of the external genitalia is unitypic (of a single type). That is, there is a single set of genitalia that has two possible destinies, namely, to become either male or female. Thus, the clitoris and the penis are homologues of one another, as are the clitoral hood and the penile foreskin. The tissues that become the labia minora in the female wrap around to become the penis in the male and fuse along the midline of the underside to form the tubular urethra. The swellings that otherwise form the divided labia majora of the female fuse in the midline to form the scrotum of the male. "The Adam principle," as applied to hormonal induction, combines the qualities of the two genitalia into one, and also the combining of the male and female pathways in the brain and its governance of the genitalia and their functioning. [148]

The primary masculinizing hormone is testosterone, although it is not necessarily used in all parts of the brain as such. Within brain cells themselves, as within cells of the pelvic genitalia, testosterone may be reduced to dihydrotestosterone (a combining of testosterone with two atoms of hydrogen). Paradoxically, it may exert its masculinizing action only if first chemically converted into estradiol (a highly estrogenic hormone), one of the sex steroids that received its name when it was considered to be exclusively an estrogenic, feminizing hormone.

Dr. Money goes on to say,

> The lateral distribution in the brain of masculine to the right and feminine to the left means that the two sides may develop to be either concordant (one masculinized and the other defeminized, or one feminized and the other demasculinized) or discordant (one masculinized and the other feminized, or one

demasculinized and the other defeminized). Disparities may come into being on the basis of the amount of hormone needed by and available to each side; the timing of its availability to each side; the synchrony or dissynchrony of the hormonal programming on each side; and the pulsatility of continuity of the hormonal supply on each side.

To sum up, dimorphic hormonalization of the prenatal brain takes place under the influence of a steroidal hormone. Normally it is testosterone, secreted by the fetal testes. Some target cells receive testosterone and change it into one of its metabolites, notably estradiol (a highly estogenic hormone) and dihydrotestosterone. This steroidal hormone masculinizes and defeminizes. Its lack or insufficiency demasculinizes and feminizes. It is possible for masculinization and feminization both to coexist to some degree, with consequent bisexual rather than monosexual manifestations of behavior. We now know that humans who are homosexual do not "prefer" to be homosexual instead of heterosexual. Nor does one choose to be bisexual or monosexual.[149]

As we have begun looking at facts, such as what homosexuality scientifically is, let us continue using reason to help us in our decision-making process. Let us start with the fact that the Bible did not always have the kind of authority that many give it today. In fact, there was no official Bible until after the Council of Trent in AD 1546. There was no Old Testament as we know it, even in the time of Jesus. This brings us to the place where we need to understand the term *canon*, what it means, and how it came about. Canon means, basically, that which is accepted, a guide or rule. In time, acceptance and use of Old Testament writings increased in authority.

Otto J. Baab, Old Testament scholar and professor at Garret School of Theology, put it this way: "Canonization is a process, rather than a decree of court or council, and in this process the literature is unconsciously subjected to severe testing as it is used to meet the personal and social needs of the group. While much of the process is unconscious, at times it is deliberately directed by writers or editors who try to adapt the biblical text to the needs of their contemporaries by inserting additions or interpolations into it. This means that, prior to the official canonization of the Old Testament books, the literature was continuously articulated with the ongoing life of the Israelite community. The writings were augmented, supplemented, and interpreted through the years so that they became both the record of the words and thoughts of their original authors and also the appropriation and adaption of these words by the continuing religious community of Israel. In as much as the life of this community retained a basic identity as it changed, the adjustments it made in biblical text through editing and rewriting tended to show the possession of a common historical faith. In this manner the canon makers, including the anonymous multitudes and the individual editors and writers, exemplified the interdependence of the community and its sacred literature. The impact of one upon the other is apparent, whether we consider the original composition of each book or its alteration through transmission and use."[150]

The first attention-getting incident that we recognize in this process of canonization of Scriptures began with Josiah. Around 700 BC, Assyria took control of Judea. Judea's kings were subservient to Assuria and allowed polytheism back then, even in the Temple. They even sacrificed their sons to Molech. This went on for some three quarters of a century. Josiah led a revolt and took back control. In doing so, part of the writing of Deuteronomy was found in a Temple wall. Josiah had it read to the people and the people agreed to have it as an official guide. This portion, if not the whole writing of Deuteronomy, became the first official Scripture. Note that it was not God who made it official, but the people.[151]

Another visible step in canonization also came about after a terrible disruption in the land. Babylon conquered Judah and there were three different deportations of Jewish leaders to Babylon in 598, 587, and 582 BC. It was not until some time after Cyrus of Persia conquered Babylon that the Judeans were free to return home. This long period of hopelessness about the present and questions about the future caused the Judeans to look back at their past and concentrate on past writings.[152] They began to look at the past writings with a different perspective and began revising many of them. It was almost 50 years before they got back home. When they went to rebuild the Temple, the Samaritans, who had not been exiled, offered to help. They were rebuffed. It was felt that since the Samaritans had not suffered the experience of the exile, they had not been purified. This led to an official break between the Judeans and Samaritans. With this break, the Samaritans kept the original five books of the law as their scriptures. They did not change them nor add other writings to them. Furthermore, they had constructed their own Temple on Mt. Gerizim.[153] This temple was destroyed in 128 BC.[154] The Pentateuch of the Samaritans remained basically the same from that point on while the Pentateuch of the Judeans was changed.

The next big development came about because of great turmoil, again, in Canaan. Due to all of the conflict, some million Jews had scattered into Egypt. The Greeks had conquered the land in about 333 BC, so most of these Jews knew Greek but no longer understood Hebrew. With their desire to have the law and other writings that had come about, some scholars set about to make a Greek translation for those around Alexandria, Egypt. The law was translated around 250 BC and other writings were finished around 75 BC.[155] These together were called The Septuagint, meaning 70, because some 70 (or 72) scholars worked at completing the translation. This translation used LORD (kurios) for Yahweh, and did not use anthropomorhisms. It also included many of the apocryphal writings. Although the Eastern and Roman Catholic canons have accepted the apocryphal writings, Protestants have not.

Somewhere around 400 BC, Ezra stood before the people and read the five books called the Pentateuch (Genesis through Deuteronomy) and all the people who gathered for the reading took a vow to have these books as their guide.[156] Once again, it took more turmoil before another development happened in the canon of Scripture. The Temple was destroyed for the last time in about AD 70. As a result, a group of rabbis set up a school at Jamnia. Some scholars tell us that these rabbis did not like the fact that Christians were using the Septuagint as Scriptures, nor how they were using them. As a result, they called a council, or Synod, in

AD 90 to do something about it. They changed the order of the writings, added some, and rejected many others. In the process of selection, several writings were heavily debated; for example, many did not want to include Ezekiel because it had too many discrepancies with the law. They did not want to include Song of Solomon because of its vulgarity. They did not want to include Ecclesiastes because it was shocking with its skepticism and irreverence, and Esther never mentioned God. However, these writings finally squeaked through.

Nevertheless, many writings, even though alluded to in the accepted writings, were rejected, such as the book of Jashar, the Book of the Wars of Yahweh, the Book of the Acts of Solomon, the Chronicles of the Kings of Judah, the Chronicles of the Kings of Israel, and the Proclamation of Josiah.

The writings that had been used as Scripture up to that time were the 39 books in the Septuagint (the Greek translation from about 250 BC). The Jamnia group changed the order of the books and added seven more, bringing the number to 46. Had these rabbis believed that the writings came from God, there is no way they would have taken it upon themselves to make the decision as to which writings were acceptable and which were not.

Other scholars, although they agree that some rabbis did meet and discuss the scriptures at Jamnia, maintain that even this meeting did not finalize the process of canonization for the Old Testament. That process went on for another century or so, even among the Jews. In fact, to this day, it still has not been agreed upon among all Christians.[157]

We must also consider the misconception that the Scriptures were translated from one original text. Our Old Testament Scriptures are assembled from parts of copies of copies of several texts from several different manuscripts that were Alexandrian, Aramaic, Masoretic, Syriac, Hebrew, the Targum, etc. What we now know as "The Old Testament" did not come from one original source. The preface and footnotes in most Bibles are very clear about this fact.

Furthermore, if you have any knowledge about translating, you know that it is impossible to translate literally from one language to another, especially from a graphic type of language like Hebrew. This means that there is no such thing as a literal translation of Scripture.

As stated above, the New Testament canon still is not agreed upon by the whole church. In 367, Bishop Athanasius sent out an Easter letter that lists the books that we Protestants now have in the New Testament as the ones he recommended. In 1442, one of the books being used as a New Testament writing was the Epistle to the Laodicians. However, the Council of Florence, which met that year and made a list of suggested texts, did not include this epistle.

At this Council, the doctrine of the inspiration of Scripture was first mentioned and it was declared that there was a unity of the Old and New Testaments. However, the list of New Testament books was not made official even at this time.

Translation and Reformation

In the 1300s, a rebellion arose against the authority of the church. John Wycliffe began preaching against the authority of the pope and transubstantiation of the communion elements. With the help of assistants, he translated the Latin Vulgate into English in 1382-84. He died in 1384, and 43 years later, church authorities dug up his bones, crushed them, burned them, and threw the remains into the Swift River. Wycliffe probably survived as long as he did because of the confusion going on in the Church. This was during the time when there were two popes, one living in Carcasone, the old city of Avignon, France, and the other in Rome. Wycliffe's followers were called the Lollards and were the precursor to the Reformation.

John Hus was a follower of Wycliffe and was burned at the stake in 1445. In 1490, Thomas Linacre, physician to the English king, learned Greek and translated the New Testament. He found that the Latin translation put forth by the church was so corrupt that he wrote in his diary, "Either this is not the Gospel, or, we are not Christians."

In 1496, John Colet translated the New Testament from Greek into English and began reading it aloud in St. Paul's Cathedral. Twenty thousand people crowded into the church and another 20,000 stood outside to hear. Copies of the Bible up until this time were made by hand. The printing press had just been invented in 1440.

By the 1500s, many groups were rebelling against the authority of the church and the pope. In 1516, Erasmus translated the Greek into Latin because he, also, had found that the Vulgate Latin translation was so faulty. Pope Leo was very angry and declared that, "The Fable of Christ was quite profitable" to him. He did not want anybody messing up his good fortune.

Both Martin Luther and Zwingly said that the Old Testament writings were not equal to those of the New Testament, and Luther went even further, saying, "the letter of the Law killeth"[158] and that we need "Faith alone."[159] In 1517, he nailed his 95 theses to the church door in Wittenberg.

In 1530, William Tyndale translated the scriptures and had them printed. He also wrote *The Obedience of Christian Man* in the same year. As punishment for printing the Bible, King Henry VIII had Tyndale strangled and burned at the stake in 1534. Ironically, the king read *The Obedience of Christian Man* two years later and used it as a basis to split the Anglican Church from the Roman Catholic Church in 1536. Even more ironic, the king had Tyndale's scriptures printed as *The Great Bible for the Church of England* in the same year. That was 75 years before the King James version was published.

Also in 1536, Luther translated both the Old and New Testaments from Greek and Hebrew into German. Although Pope Damasus had insisted in the 900s that there were 46 books in the Old Testament, Martin used the 39 in the Septuagint. Seven people were burned at the stake in that year for disagreeing with the Church.

My mother was a Rogers. While working on my genealogy, I discovered that John Rogers printed the first Bible translated entirely from the Hebrew and Greek into English in 1537. He, also, was burned at the stake by Queen Mary for doing so. His wife and 10 children stood by watching.

The Church was losing control. The pope called for the Council of Trent to combat the problem. This council met on and off for 18 years and one major project was to come up with an official list of books for the Bible. This Council ended in 1546. All the above translations had occurred before there was an official, church-recognized Bible.

Contrary to popular belief, our Scriptures did not have the authority that they are given today for three quarters of our church history. The church had the authority, not the Scriptures, except as the church interpreted the scriptures.

In the earliest days of the Christian Church, there came to be literally hundreds, if not thousands, of documents written, all purporting to be scriptural. It was the church, which came to be known as the Catholic (meaning "universal") Church, that designated which of these writings were to be considered valid, or as we call it, the inspired canon. The writings in the Bible were selected from many writings through the years by various groups.

In the process of selecting the scriptures to be canonized to form the New Testament, the Council of Trent argued for a long time over whether or not to include Revelation because so much of it varied from Jesus' teachings. They also rejected many of the writings that had been in use, including the Gospel Q, Gospel of Mary, Gospel of Thomas, Secret Book of James, Dialogue of the Savior, Infancy Gospel of Thomas, Infancy Gospel of James, Egerton Gospel, Gospel of the Hebrews, Gospel of the Ebionites, Gospel of the Nazoreans, and the Gospel Oxythynthus. Those at the Council of Trent were not even aware of the Gospel of Judas. The Greek Church and the Gothic Church (non-Trinitarian) have only 22 books in their New Testament. We Protestants have 27.

How can we come to a true understanding of what is meant by the Word of God if we do not know more about the writings that make up our Bible? What does it say to us that the first half of our Old Testament background involved not only polytheism, but fertility cult worship as well? And then, for several centuries, our Old Testament history included monolateralism, one God among many gods.

As for me, I do believe that there has always been only one God. It was not God who changed; it was people's understanding of God that changed. People relate differently depending on how they view God; just as people's ideas about marriage—good, bad, and evil—change as their knowledge and understandings change.

What one believes about God is life changing and action changing. One thing that does not change is the effects of being judgmental. Wanting to play God has dire consequences, whether eating from the judgment tree in the Garden of Eden, putting Jesus on the cross for blasphemy, or condemning people today. We can center on law, and thus on condemnation, or follow Christ who taught that love, forgiveness, and reconciliation is God's way, not condemnation and judgment.

We really do need to explore what the Word of God means for us as we consider the issue of homosexuality. We especially need to understand that, because of the complicating factors shared above, along with peoples' various experiences, "the Word of God" has different meanings for different people.

Despite Jesus', Paul's, and Wesley's warnings about the evil of the condemnation of others, our Discipline of the United Methodist Church states, "Homosexuality is incompatible with Christian teaching."[160] This statement has given many the excuse to condemn homosexuals. However, because of what we have learned from Scripture, tradition, and experience, the only way to come to that conclusion is by using faulty doctrines that started with Origen and Augustine and culminated with Aquinas' so-called natural law. As we have explored, there is nothing in Scripture, or the teachings of Jesus, or the first 1200 years of official church history and tradition that provides any such teaching about same-sex relationships.

As Christians, we follow the teachings of Jesus, the Christ, who never taught anything against same-sex relationships. I have asked several bishops to show me or tell me where I can find Christian teachings that show opposition to homosexuality. None could do so. Our denomination has fallen into the trap of calling a faulty church doctrine based on a faulty concept (that of "Natural Law") a "Christian teaching." Not only is the Doctrine faulty, but we are not a doctrinal church. This opposition is certainly not a teaching of Jesus. One of the things in connection with our branch of Christianity of which I am most proud is John Wesley's approach to doctrine and Christianity. Let me summarize this approach as it is stated in the United Methodist Book of Discipline.

Doctrinal Standards

We share a common heritage with Christians of every age and nation. This heritage is grounded in the apostolic witness to Jesus Christ as savior and Lord, which is the source and soundness of all Christian teaching.[161]

The Protestant reformers of the 16th and 17th centuries devised new confessional statements that reiterated classical Christian teaching in an attempt to recover the authentic biblical witness.[162] In other words, the reformers, including John Wesley, did not see as binding the doctrines that had been accumulating through church history nor the kind of authority that the Church had come to demand. The Scriptures are the primary guide, as interpreted through the teachings of Jesus. That is our doctrinal standard.

As Christians we (Methodists) affirm that:[163]

1. The created order is designed for the well-being of all creatures, and as the place of human dwelling in covenant with God.

2. Through faith in Jesus Christ, we are forgiven, reconciled to God, and transformed as people of the New Covenant.

3. We share with many Christian communions a recognition of the authority of Scripture in matters of faith, and the sober realization that the church is in continual need of reformation and renewal.

4. The underlying energy of the Wesleyan theological heritage stems from an emphasis upon practical divinity, which is the implementation of genuine Christianity in the lives of believers.

5. Our task is not to reformulate doctrine. Our task is to summon people to experience the justifying and sanctifying grace of God and to encourage people to grow in the knowledge and love of God through the personal and corporate disciplines of the Christian life.

6. Wesley's orientation toward the practical is evident in his focus upon "the scripture way of salvation." He considered doctrinal

matters primarily in their significance for Christian discipleship, not church law.

7. The Wesleyan emphasis upon the Christian life—faith and love put into practice—has been the hallmark of those traditions.

The distinctive Wesleyan emphasis is:

Grace pervades the understanding of Christian faith and life. We must ask ourselves, have we received grace? Do we treat others with this kind of love, grace? Do we see unworthy persons the way God sees them, with grace? If God does not see persons as "unworthy," why do we judge others to be unworthy? Christian experience as personal transformation always presents itself as faith working by love—anything else is not Christian.

Sanctification and perfection means:

1. We hold that the wonder of God's acceptance and pardon does not end God's saving work, which continues to nurture our growth in grace. Through the power of the Holy Spirit, we are enabled to increase in the knowledge and love of God and love for our neighbor. This love grows; it does not stagnate or regress.

2. New birth is the first step in this process of sanctification. Sanctifying grace draws us toward the gift of Christian perfection, which Wesley described as a heart "habitually filled with the love of God and neighbor," and as "having the mind of Christ and walking as he walked."

3. Faith is the only response needed for salvation. There is no other test.

4. Scriptural holiness entails more than personal piety; love of God is always linked with love of neighbor, a passion for justice, and renewal in the life of the world.

5. For Wesley there is no religion but social religion and no holiness but social holiness. Our personal growth is for mission and service to others. That is the telling mark of whether one is a Christian or not. The coherence of faith with ministries of love forms the discipline of Wesleyan spirituality and Christian discipleship.

Wesley insisted that evangelical faith should manifest itself in evangelical living. He spelled out this expectation in a three part formula: "It is therefore expected that all who continue therin, that they should continue to evidence their desire for salvation,

"First, by doing no harm by, avoiding evil of every kind...

"Secondly...by doing good of every possible sort, and, as far as possible, to all...

"Thirdly, by attending upon all the ordinances of God," which includes his Doctrinal Standards (as presented above).[164] However, Wesley rejected undue reliance upon even these rules. Discipline was not church law; it was a guide for discipleship.

These distinctive emphases provide the basis for practical divinity, the experiential realization of the gospel of Jesus Christ in the lives of Christian people. Wesley centered on Scripture and faith, not on doctrines of the church. As Wesley put it, "As to all opinions that do not strike at the root of Christianity, we think and let think."[165] Those who brought about the Reformation reaffirmed the ancient creeds and confessions as valid summaries of Christian truth. But they were careful not to set them apart as absolute standards for doctrinal truth and error. Wesley followed a time-tested approach: "In essentials, unity; in non-essentials, liberty; and in all things, charity."[166] The spirit of charity takes into consideration the limits of human understanding.

"To be ignorant in many things and to be mistaken in some," Wesley observed, "is the necessary condition of humanity."[167] The crucial matter in religion is steadfast love for God and neighbor, empowered by the redeeming and sanctifying work of the Holy Spirit. Wesley never reduced theology to a confessional formula as a doctrinal test. The Bible constituted for him the final authority in all doctrinal matters. There was no other doctrine.

In fact, Wesley's preface to his *Articles of Religion* states, "These are the doctrines taught among the people called Methodists. Nor is there any doctrine whatever, generally received, among that people, contrary to the articles now before you." Furthermore, even of the articles of religion and rules for the church that Wesley set forward, he stated, "The doctrinal emphases of these statements were carried forward by the weight of tradition rather than the force of law."[168] "Whatever is not revealed in or established by the holy Scriptures is not to be made an article of faith nor is it to be taught as essential to salvation."[169]

There was nothing at all about homosexuality revealed in holy Scripture; therefore, it has absolutely nothing to do with salvation. Our theological task is both critical and constructive. It is critical in that we test various expressions of faith by asking, Are they true? Appropriate?

Clear? Cogent? Credible? Are they based on love? Do they provide the Church and its members with a witness that is faithful to the gospel as reflected in our living heritage and that is authentic and convincing in the light of human experience and the present state of human knowledge?[170]

The statement we have in our Discipline now about homosexuality is not true, is not credible, and certainly is not the most loving thing to do. It breaks every one of the Methodist standards for a constructive theological criterion. We are to interpret individual texts in light of their place in the Bible as a whole, Wesley said.[171] But that is not what our church is doing today on this issue, nor has it done so for the last 40 years. We, the church, have betrayed scripture, the teachings of Jesus, and John Wesley's concept of Christianity.

Wesley said, "The history of Christianity includes a mixture of ignorance, misguided zeal, and sin. Scripture remains the norm by which all traditions are judged. All religious experience affects all human experience; all human experience affects our understanding of all religious experience. Christian experience gives us new eyes to see the living truth in scripture."[172] Too often, theology is used to support practices that are unjust. We look for answers that are in harmony with the gospel and do not claim exemption from critical assessment.[173]

The reformers, including Wesley, wanted an end to inquisitions in the Church. But we have not learned. We are led by something other than the teachings of Jesus and the Scriptures. We do not pay attention to present day knowledge and we pay little attention to experience. We seem to have lost our ability to reason.

Jesus said in Matthew 7:1f, "Do not judge that you may not be judged. For with the judgment you make, you will be judged, and the measure you give will be the measure you get. Why do you see the speck in your neighbor's eye but do not notice the log in your own eye? Or, how can you say to your neighbor, "Let me take the speck out of your eye," while the log is in your own eye? You hypocrite, take the log out of your own eye and then you will see clearly to take the speck out of your neighbor's eye."

Scriptures tell us that all sins are bad and that all people sin. When did we start picking out one that is worse than others? If you consider homosexuality a sin, is that sin greater than yours? Our first concern should be about our own sin, not that of someone else.

The struggle to know God is the story of the Old Testament. Charles Wesley, John's brother and the greatest hymn writer in history, responded to that quest by taking Jacob's experience at the Jabbock River and answering Jacob's request, "Please, tell me your name." Recall the incident in Genesis 32:24-30 and remember how and why Jacob got his name. When he was born, he had hold of his twin brother's heel. He wanted to be first, thus he was given the name Jacob, "Supplanter." He was self-centered, a conniver who wanted to be number one. He later tricked his father into giving him his brother's inheritance.

In this part of the story, Jacob was alone with his guilty conscience and he wrestled a man (God) until daybreak. Then the one he wrestled said, "Let me go for the day is breaking."

But Jacob said, "I will not let you go unless you bless me."

So the man said to Jacob, "What is your name?"

"Jacob," he replied.

Then the man said, "You will no longer be called Jacob, but Israel. For you have striven with God and with humans, and have prevailed."

Then Jacob said, "Please tell me your name."

Charles Wesley used this incident in the Old Testament to describe the search to know God and related it to the coming of Jesus. Wesley responded to Jacob's question "What is your name?" with his hymn, "Come, O Thou Traveler Unknown."

> Come, O thou traveler unknown
> whom still I hold but cannot see.
> My company before is gone
> And I am left alone with thee.
>
> I need not tell thee who I am
> my misery and sin declare.
> Thyself has called me by my name,
> look on thy hands and read it there.
>
> Yield to me now for I am weak
> but confident in self despair!
> Speak to my heart, in blessing speak,
> be conquered by my instant prayer.
>
> 'Tis love, 'tis love, thou diedst for me,
> I hear thy whisper in my heart,
> the morning breaks, the shadows flee,

pure, universal love thou art.

The answer is universal love, God's love for all revealed by Jesus.

Regarding the Bible, we have learned that the Scriptures include dynamic, revealing, developing concepts. They are not locked in time. The writers were not afraid to put into plain view where they were in their relationship to the holy, and that those views changed. They were not afraid to reveal the development in their faith process. They show us clearly their development from polytheism through monolateralism to monotheism: a development from belief in many supernatural powers, each labeled a god or goddess; to an awesome, distant, fearful God who was superior to other gods; to the one and only God who loves and cares for us all.

The writers also reveal changes in marriage customs. After some thousand years of polygamy, they changed to monogamy. They went from marrying within the family (sister, cousins, etc.) to outside the family.

The writers show us very clearly that they could not produce righteous living by following laws, rules, and regulations. As the prophets stated again and again, the Old Covenant established on laws did not work; it was a system of judging others that did not result in righteous living. The authority gained from the Old Testament is in its witness to the divine activity of God in people's lives and situations.

This history prepared the people for the coming of Christ. The coming of Christ put an end to the period of preparation and began a New Covenant. From the Garden story, organized around the judgment tree in the Old Covenant, to the coming of Jesus, who insisted that we are not to judge others, we are taught that judgment is not God's way.

Judgment ends in terrible atrocities such as stoning people to death; putting someone as innocent as Jesus on a torturous cross; killing Stephen, Peter and Paul; the crusades; inquisitions; burning people at the stake; and labeling some people as outcasts just because of who they are. In the Old Testament, lepers and Samaritans were unworthy. Today it is homosexuals, or conservatives, or liberals, or others depending on where one stands theologically.

God's message to us, through Jesus, reveals that we are to care for one another, to be good neighbors—love God and love others as ourselves. In connection with this, we would do well to remember that it was not Jesus who brought up the question about being saved. This issue of salvation came about because Jesus was asked what one must do to be saved. That discourse ended with Jesus answering, "Be a good neighbor."

"But who is my neighbor?" The questioner wanted specifics. Jesus' answer was in the parable of the Good Samaritan. Now, you and I know that in those days, there was no such thing as a good Samaritan. Samaritans were considered so unworthy that one was not even to step into their territory. Yet Jesus used the example of such a person as providing the way to salvation. The lawyer asked the wrong question. He was looking in the wrong direction. Salvation is not self- centered. Any follower of Jesus, like you and me, is to be a good neighbor. We are to help those in need—the hungry, the thirsty, the sick—we are to forgive and reconcile whomever is in need; to free the oppressed. The way to salvation certainly is not to become oppressors ourselves.

The New Covenant is to be carried forward by the Christian fellowship of the *eklesia*, meaning "people called out" to care for others in the way that Jesus cares for all. That is what "church" really means. Jesus did not come for one's selfish personal salvation. Jesus came to reveal behavior as loving, forgiving, reconciling, and living as a good neighbor. We are not to judge or to condemn anyone. We are sent out to be redeemers. "As my Father has sent me, so send I you," said Jesus (John 20:21). They will know we are Christians by our love, the love of Christ, the love of God.

We function by grace, not by law. But, what is this grace? We use the word grace so much that it almost becomes meaningless. The secular term means basically "favor" or "thanks." And in the Old Testament, it is favor or reward that has been earned by sustained obedience. However, in the New Testament, and particularly as used some 101 times by Paul, grace is very different. The grace that Jesus revealed is a free gift of mercy, freedom from guilt; it is not earned and it is given to the undeserving. Jesus extended grace to the unworthy.

Recall Jesus and the Samaritan woman at Jacob's well. According to the law, Jesus should not have even spoken to her. He knew about all the men in her life and the fact that she was not married to the one with whom she was living at the time. He did not condemn her. In fact, because of his approach, she became the first evangelist. She went to the very people who looked down upon her and invited them to come and hear what Jesus had to say.

Grace pervades the understanding of Christian faith and life. And this is the huge difference in Christianity. Jesus expects as much from his followers. Paul tells us in Romans 12 and 1 Corinthians 13 that God gives gifts of grace *charismata*: prophecy, service, exhortation, teaching, etc. But the greatest gift is love. We are to use our gifts for the benefit of others.

We must ask ourselves, have we received grace? Do we treat others with this kind of love, grace? Obviously, God does not see people as unworthy. Why do we judge others as unworthy, incompatible? Jesus showed that God is far more compassionate than man.

The authority that we see in the work of the apostles is not of the magisterial kind, working by dictation and coercion, but rather it is a kind that works through love, as we see in the parable of the Good Samaritan, the parable of the Lost Sheep, Jesus with the Samaritan woman at the well, and Jesus speaking up for the woman caught in adultery. We see it in Jesus' prayer for those who had him condemned and tortured to death, saying "Father, forgive them; they know not what they do."

It is a grave disloyalty to Christ to use the kind of authority, or a system of doctrine, that expects others to earn salvation. That is no different from the way the Scribes and Pharisees were using the Old Testament writings.[174] Our authority is when Christ's truth becomes our truth, when Christ's purpose is fulfilled in our living.

The authority of scripture does not come from its infallibility or inerrancy, but from its revelation of God at work in our lives.

Ironically, when we look up Scripture to evaluate, judge, and condemn others, we are doing the very opposite of what Jesus taught. This is identical to the method of the Scribes and Pharisees. We participate in the very same type of religion that put Jesus to death. When we do this, we reveal that we have not learned one thing about the gospel or the purpose of Christianity. We betray Christ.

Ironically, too many of the concepts behind so-called orthodox Christian teachings are merely was of practicing another brand of Phariseeism. While posing as a guardian of Christ's teachings, these doctrines, in fact, abandon Christ's teachings and become instruments to separate, divide, condemn. It is the same old, same old. In this case, to take texts referring to fertility cult worship and apply them to same-sex relationships is not only a deplorable misuse of Scripture, it is a denial of the way of Christ. It is a betrayal of Christ.

Our church history shows clearly that, from the first Church Council in about AD 49 until the 1200s, the church protected same-sex relationships rather than opposed them. Because of the adoption of Origen and Augustine's doctrines (which had nothing to do with what the scriptures revealed) the church has had problems with the very act of sex ever since, believing wrongly that sex passed on sin and was only for procreation.

The Church has totally neglected the original story of creation, which centered on companionship. Instead, it has centered on procreation from the story that was intended to emphasize the importance of the Sabbath. In fact, the church has practically turned this story into a false, anti-sexual doctrine. We have betrayed both the Scriptures and the teachings of Jesus.

Almost all of the sexual issues faced in our church history have been based on the concept of the misuse of sperm, and this has little if any relationship to Scripture. And, to be honest, the church has been far more concerned with marital relationships, chastity, and celibacy than with same-sex relationships.

For the last 700 years, same-sex behavior has been evaluated under the guise of a doctrine of "natural law." The prime author of the doctrine of natural law was Thomas Aquinas in his treatise *Summa Theologie*. And in that very same treatise, he wrote that if it were shown that same-sex relationships were natural, there would be nothing wrong with them. For well over a half a century now we have had that proof that homosexuality is natural. People are born that way. If one takes Thomas Aquinas as the church's ultimate authority on such issues, rather than Scripture and the teachings of Jesus, why not read and use his entire treatise, not just part of it?

There is apparently more involved in many people's decision concerning the relationship of Christianity to homosexuals than what is presented in the Bible, in Christian tradition, and, certainly, in the facts about sexual orientation. If we stuck to these sources, it would be very clear that homosexuals are as much a part of God's creation and loved ones as any of us. Instead, we have betrayed the true teachings.

What part does your theology play? Have you analyzed your theology and do you understand why you have your kind of theology? Are you a literalist, conservative, liberal, or more towards humanism? Probably no one fits exactly into any of these labels. I, for example, would like to think that I am, like Jesus, liberal. However, I am a stickler for accurate literal translation of Scripture. It really bothers me that even the best translations at times include biases rather than the original meanings.

With regard to homosexuality, we now know beyond the shadow of a doubt that it is biological, natural, not a preference, not a choice; with the result that all the teaching and praying in the world is not going to change that fact. Homosexuals are as worthy as I am or as anyone else is. As for me, I want to follow Christ. Christians do not sow dissension, do not oppress; they reconcile. Where do you stand?

May God be with you, and you with God.

Bibliography

Baab, Otto J. *Theology of the Old Testament*. Nashville, TN: Abingdon Press, 1953.

Bailey, Derrick Sherwin. *Homosexuality and the Western Christian Tradition*. London, 1955.

Book of Discipline of the United Methodist Church. Nashville, TN: The United Methodist Publishing House, 2000.

Boswell, John. *Christianity, Social Tolerance and Homosexuality: Gay People in Western Europe from the Beginning of the Christian Era to the Fourteenth Century*. Chicago: University of Chicago Press, 1981.

Brawley, Robert L. *Biblical Ethics and Homosexuality*. Louisville, KY: Westminster John Knox Press, 1996.

Buttrick, George Arthur, ed. *The Interpreters Bible*, Nashville, TN: Abingdon Press, 1953.

Buttrick, George Arthur, ed. *The Interpreters Dictionary of the Bible*, Nashville, TN: Abingdon Press, 1962.

Cameron, Alan. *Circus Factions: Blues and Greens at Rome and Byzantium*. New York: Oxford University Press, 1976.

De Lille, Alain. *The Complaint of Nature*, translated by Douglas Moffat. New York: Henry Holt & Co., 1908.

Durand, Alfred. "Inspiration of the Bible." *The Catholic Encyclopedia*. New York: Robert Appleton Company, 1913.

Economou, George. *The Goddess Natura in Medieval Literature*. Cambridge, MA: University of Notre Dame Press, 1972.

Eiselen, Brederick Carl, ed. *The Abingdon Bible Commentary*. Nashville, TN: Abingdon Press, 1928.

Geisler, Norman L., ed. *Inerrancy*. Grand Rapids, MI: Zondervan, 1980.

Gottwald, Norman K. *A Light to the Nations*. New York: Harper and Brothers, 1959.

Grudem, Wayne A. *Systematic theology: an introduction to biblical doctrine*. Leicester, UK: Inter-Varsity Press, 1994.

Haiken, Alex. "When the Presumptions of Men Obscure the Truth of Scripture." https://jewishchristiangay.wordpress.com/2012/09/23/when-presumptions-of-men-obscure-the-truth-of-scripture/

Holy Bible, Revised Standard Edition, 1946, 1952.

Jewish Encyclopedia sv. Inspiration. http://www.jewishencyclopedia.com/articles/8126-inspiration

Keating, Karl. "Proving Inspiration." *Catholic Answers*, 2004. http://www.catholic.com/tracts/proving-inspiration

Kroeger, Catherine. "The Apostle Paul and the Greco-Roman Cults of Women." *Journal of the Evangelical Theological Society* 30/1 (1987): 25–38.

Lambert, M. D. *Franciscan Poverty: The Doctrine of Absolute Poverty of Christ and the Apostles in the Franciscan Order, 1210-1323*. St. Bonaventure, NY: The Franciscan Institute, 1998.

Metzger, Bruce. *The Canon of the New Testament*. Oxford, UK: Clarendon Press, 1987.

Metzger, Bruce M., and Michael D. Coogan, eds. *The Oxford Companion to the Bible*. New York, NY: Oxford University Press, 1993.

Wright, Thomas, ed. *The Anglo-Latin Satirical Poets and Epigrammatists of the Twelfth Century.* London, 1872.

Notes

PL = Patrologiae Cursus Completus, Series Latina

PG = Patrologiae Cursus Completus, Series Graeca

Chapter 3

1. Jewish Encyclopedia sv. Inspiration, v. 4, 607.

2. Ibid, 608.

3. Jn. 4:3-42.

4. Ex. 20:17 (in the Samaritan Pentateuch); Deut. 27:4-8; Joshua 5:9-15; 21:25-5-26.

5. 1 Sam. 25:25.

6. Metzger, *The Canon of the New Testament*, 254.

7. Metzger & Coogan, *The Oxford Companion to the Bible*, 302-304.

8. Durand, "Inspiration of the Bible" in *The Catholic Encyclopedia*, 3.

9. Born 1950, Keating is a prominent Catholic apologist and author, the founder and president of Catholic Answers, and a lay apostolate of Catholic apologetics and evangelization.

10. Myers, *The Eerdmans Dictionary of the Bible*, "inspiration," 641.

11. Ibid.

12. Ibid.

13. Ibid.

14. Lea & Griffin, Vol. 34: 1, 2 Timothy, Titus. *The New American Commentary*, 239.

15. Ibid.

16. Keating, "Proving Inspiration," *Catholic Answers*.

17. Grudem, *Systematic Theology*, 90.

18. McKim, *Westminster Dictionary*, p. 2; Geisler, *Inerrancy*, 22.

19. Buttrick, *Interpreter's Bible*, Vol.1, 166.

20. Mk. 7:12 f.

Chapter 4

21. Ex. 24:4; 24:12; 34:1; 34:27-28.

22. Buttrick, *Interpreter's Dictionary of the Bible*, Vol. E-J:754.

23. Buttrick, *Interpreter's Bible*, Vol. 1:34.

24. Ibid, 34-35.

25. Ibid, 35.

26. Ibid.

27. Eiselen, *Abingdon Bible Commentary*, 41

28. Buttrick, *Interpreter's Bible*, Vol. 1: 39.

29. Ibid.

30. Mk. 7:1-13.

31. Gottwald, *A Light to the Nations*, 107-112.

32. Buttrick, *Interpreter's Bible*, Vol. 1:726.

33. Buttrick, *Interpreter's Dictionary of the Bible*, Vol. E-J:751, 1003

34. Money, "Sin, Sickness, or Status," *American Psychologist*, 42/4: 384-399.

Chapter 5

35. Boswell, *Christianity, Social Tolerance, and Homosexuality*, 100-101.
    Addresses Sanhedrin 7.4.53A and Maimonides' Code 5.1.14.

36. Brawley, *Biblical Ethics and Homosexuality*, 19.

37. Ibid, 26

38. Acts 11:2.

39. Acts 11:3.

40. Lk. 15:2.

41. Gal. 1:9.

42. Gal. 5:1-2.

43. Romans 3:20.

44. Romans 2:1-3:30.

45. Kroeger, "The Apostle Paul and the Greco-Roman Cults of Women," *Journal of the Evangelical Theological Society*, 30/1:37

46. Hellenica 3.4.19; 6.1.6; Apology 19; Memorabilia 1.2.2.

47. Boswell, 106, footnote 50. Addresses *Cynic Epistles*.

48. *Roman Antiquities* 7.2.4.

49. Cassius 58.4.6; Plutarch, *Pericles*, 27.4; Josephus, *War*, 6.211, *Antiquities* 19.197.).

50. Aquinas, *Summa Theologiae*, 2.2.154.11

51. Beauvais, *Speculum Doctrinale*, 107, 4.162.

52. Josephus, *War*, 7.338; *Antiquities*, 5.246; 10.194.

53. Chrysostom, 66.25

54. Aristotle, *Nicomachean Ethics* 7.4.4

55. Plutarch, *Erotikos* 753; cf. 751

56. Boswell, 55.

57. Boswell, 351. Addresses Chrysostom, *In Epistolam ad Romanos*, homily 4, PG 60:415-22.

58. Haiken, Alex. "When the Presumptions of Men Obscure the Truth of Scripture." Reprinted with permission of the author.

59. Buttrick, *Interpreter's Dictionary of the Bible*, Vol. E-J:3.

60. Buttrick, *Interpreter's Bible*, Vol. 1:3-5.

Chapter 6

61. Jn. 3:17; Jn. 8:15.

62. Lk. 6:37; Romans 2:1f.

63. Romans 8:34.

64. Jn. 8:1-20.

65. Lev. 20:10; Deut.22:22.

66. Romans 5: 12-18.

67. 1 Corinthians 11:32.

68. Acts 1.

69. Read Romans and Galatians.

70. Boswell, 131. Addresses Tacitus, *Annal* 15-44; Pliny, *Epistles* 10.96; and Minucius Felix's *Octavius* Ch. 28; as presented in Noonan, John. *Contraception: A History of Its Treatment by the Catholic Theologians and Canonists*. Cambridge, MA, 1965.

71. Ibid, 165. Addresses Augustine, *Summa contra gentiles* 3:124.

72. Ibid, 128.

73. Ibid, 109. Addresses Chrysostom, *In Epistolum ad Romans*.

74. Ibid, 133-134.

75. Boswell, 156. Addresses Chrysostom, *Contra mendacium* 7:10; PL 40:496.

76. Boswell, 154. Addresses Plutarch, *Moralia*.

77. Ibid, 164. Addresses Justin Martyr, *1 Apology*, 29.

78. Ibid. Addresses Vincent of Beauvais, *Speculum doctrinale*, 10:45.

79. Ibid. Addresses Augustine, *Soliloquia*, 1.40, PL 32:878.

80. Ibid, 172. Addresses Johannes Malalas, *Chronographia*, 18.168, PG 97:644, and Procopius, *The Anecodota*, 11:13f.

81. Ibid, 173. Addresses Procopius, 11:13f. Cameron, 16:23-28.

82. Cameron, 16:23-28.

83. Boswell, 174.

84. Bailey, *Homosexuality and the Western Christian Tradition*, 93. Addresses

Legas Visigothorum, Suppl. (MGH), 483.

85. Boswell, 180, footnote 38. Addresses *31 Mansi*, 12:295.

86. Ibid, 177. Addresses *Lex Salica, 100 Titel,* Text ed. K.A. Eckhardt, Weimar, 1953, and other references.

87. Ibid, 177, footnote 27.

88. Ibid, 177, footnote 30.

89. Ibid, 182. Addresses MGH, Legas, 3. Concilia, 2.2. p. 635.

90. Boswell, 202. Addresses St. Boniface, *De ecclesiasticus discipinis libri duo,* 2.249, 246, PL 132:322.

91. Ibid, 203. Addresses John Devisse, *Hincmar, archevegue de Reims, 845-882* (Geneva, 1975-76), 3 vols. col. 693.

92. Ibid, 203. Addresses Hadden & Stubbs, *Councils and Ecclesiastical Documents relating to Great Britain and Ireland.* Oxford, 1871, 3:354.

93. Ibid, 205. Addresses Burchard of Worms, *Decretorum libri XX*, Liber 19.

94. Ryan, *Saint Peter Damiani and his Canonical Sources*, 155.

95. Boswell, 211-212.

96. Little, "The Personal Development of Peter Damian," in *Order and Innovation in the Middle Ages*, 333-334.

97. Ibid, 334

98. Boswell, 213. Addresses correspondence of Ivo of Chartres, translation by Jean Leclerog, Paris, 1949. Vol 1, nos. 65-66, and *Allia Christiana*, 8.1441-46, etc.

99. Ibid, 214.

100. Ibid, 21. Addresses Fliche, *Le regne*, 441-442.

101. Bailey, 124-125.

102. Ibid.

103. Boswell, 217.

104. Ibid, 218.

105. Ibid, 227-228. Addresses Peter Lombard, *Sententiarum Libri Quatuor,* 4-38.4, PL 192:933.

106. Ibid, p. 274.

107. Ibid.

108. Lambert. *Franciscan Poverty,* 235-236.

109. Ibid, 276.

110. Wright, *Anglo-Latin Satirical Poets and Epigrammatists.* 138.

111. Ibid. Addresses Cantor, *Verbum abbreviatum,* PL 205:335.

112. Boswell, 277-278. Addresses Mansi, 22:224-225.

113. Ibid, 278. Addresses *Decretalium Gregorii Papae II,* 3.1.13.

114. Bailey, 96. Addresses *Mansi,* 21:264.

115. Boswell, 282. Addresses William of Ada, *De modo Sarracenos exterpandi, in Recueil des historiens des crusades: documents armeniens* (Paris, 1869-1906) 2:524 and 524-525.

116. Ibid, 283.

117. Ibid, 288.

118. Ibid, 293.

119. Ibid.

120. Ibid, 294. Addresses *Le Liber de excommunicacione du Cardinal Berenger Fredol,* ed. Eugene Vernay (Paris,1912), 4:14.

121. Ibid, 304, footnote 3.

122. Ibid, 305. Addresses Damian, *De bono religiosi status et variarum anamatium Tropologia 2,* PL 145:767.

123. Ibid. Addresses *De bono 12,* 777-78; *19,* 780.

124. Ruska, *Turba philosophorum,* Vol. 1:324-327.

125. Boswell, 309. Addresses Morlaix, *De contemptu mundi,* p.80 Line 4; p.81 Line 3

126. Ibid. Addresses Vincent of Beauvais, *Speculum doctrinale.*

127. De Lille, *The Complaint of Nature*.

128. Boswell, 311. Addresses Economou, *The Goddess Natura*.

129. Ibid, 312.

130. Ibid, 313.

131. Ibid, 316.

132. Ibid.

133. Ibid, 316-317.

134. Ibid, 319.

135. Ibid, 321. Addressses *Summa Theolgiae* 2a.2ae.154-2 and 6.

136. Ibid, 322. Addresses *Summa Theologiae*, 1a, 2ae. 31.7; 94.3 ad 2; 2.a.2ae.154-11-12.

137. Ibid.

138. Ibid.

139. Ibid, 331. Addresses *Summa Theolgiae*.137; *Panormitenus Commentaria*, T.180.

140. Brawley, 130.

Chapter 7

141. Money, "Sin, Sickness, or Status," *American Psychologist 47/*4:384-389.

142. Ibid.

143. Masters & Johnson, 409.

144. Ibid.

145. Ibid.

146. Ibid.

147. Ibid, 386.

148. Ibid, 387.

149. Ibid, 384.

150. Baab, *Theology of the Old Testament*, 253.

151. Gottwald, 326f.

152. Ibid, 331-334.

153. Ibid, 435.

154. Buttrick, *Interpreter's Bible*, Vol. 1:35.

155. Gottwald, 49f.

156. Nehemiah 8-10:30.

157. Eiselen, 97-98.

158. Luther, *Sermons*, Vol. 8:224.

159. Bouman, "The Doctrine of Justification in the Lutheran Confessions," *Concordia Theological Monthly* 26 (November 1955) No. 11:801.

160. United Methodist Church, "Qualifications for Ordination," http://www.umc.org/what-we-believe/homosexuality-full-book-of-discipline-statements

161. *Book of Discipline*, 41-42.

162. Ibid, 42.

163. Ibid, 43 and ff.

164. Ibid, 65-69.

165. United Methodist Church, "Section 2: Our Doctrinal History," http://www.umc.org/what-we-believe/section-2-our-doctrinal-history

166. Ibid.

167. Ibid.

168. *Book of Discipline*, 53.

169. Ibid, 67.

170. Ibid, 75.

171. Ibid, 78.

172. Ibid, 81.

173. Ibid, 83.

174. Buttrick, *Interpreter's Bible*, Vol. 7:25.